MANDELA

MANDELA:

THE MAN, THE STRUGGLE, THE TRIUMPH

BY DOROTHY & THOMAS HOOBLER

FRANKLIN WATTS
NEW YORK   LONDON   TORONTO   SYDNEY

Quotations from *Part of My Soul Went with Him,* by Winnie Mandela, edited by Anne Benjamin and adapted by Mary Benson, are reprinted with the permission of W.W. Norton & Co., Inc. Copyright © 1984 by Rowohlt Taschenbuch Verlag GmbH, Reinbek bei Hamburg. All rights reserved. First American Edition 1985.

Quotations from *Nelson Mandela, The Man and the Movement,* by Mary Benson, are reprinted by the permission of W.W. Norton & Co., Inc. Copyright © 1986 by Mary Benson.

Excerpts from *Higher Than Hope* by Fatima Meer, are reprinted by permission of HarperCollins Pubs. and Sheil Land Assoc., Ltd. Copyright 1990 by Fatima Meer.

The poem by Zindzi Mandela, from *Black As I Am,* Los Angeles: Guild of Tutors Press of International College, 1978.

Map by Vantage Art

Insert photographs copyright ©: AP/Wide World Photos: pp. 1, 4 bottom, 5 top, 7, 9 top, 13, 14 top; Impact Visuals: pp. 2 (Eli Weinberg/IDAF), 9 bottom (Anna Zieminski), 11 (Peter Auf Der Heyde), 16 (Roger Bosch); Gamma-Liaison: pp. 3 (Mohamed Lounes), 4 top, 6 (William Knosi), 15 (Guy Hobbs); Archive Photos, NYC: p. 5 bottom (LDE); UPI/Reuters/Bettmann: pp. 8, 10, 12, 14 bottom.

Library of Congress Cataloging-in-Publication Data

Hoobler, Dorothy.
Mandela   34
by Dorothy and Thomas Hoobler.
p.   cm.
Includes bibliographical references and index.
Summary: A biography of South African human rights activist, Nelson Mandela.
ISBN 0-531-11141-5 (lib. bdg.). — ISBN 0-531-15245-6 (trade)
1. Mandela, Nelson, 1918-   —Juvenile literature.   2. Civil rights workers—South Africa—Biography—Juvenile literature.
3. African National Congress—Biography—Juvenile literature.
4. Anti-apartheid movements—South Africa—Biography—Juvenile literature.   5. Political prisoners—South Africa—Biography—Juvenile literature.   6. South Africa—Biography—Juvenile literature. [1. Mandela, Nelson, 1918- . 2. Civil rights workers.   3. Blacks—South Africa—Biography.] I. Hoobler, Thomas.
II. Title.
DT1949.M35H36   1991
968.06′4′092—dc20
[B]
91-36649   CIP   AC

 # CONTENTS

Introduction
9

1
"I Listened to Elders of Our Tribe"
11

2
A Young Man in Johannesburg
22

3
"No Easy Walk to Freedom"
32

4
The Treason Trial
46

5
The Black Pimpernel
57

6
A Life Sentence
68

7
Prisoner Number 446/64
76

8
A Name That Would Not Die
85

9
Free Mandela!
96

10
Freedom
108

11
A New South Africa
119

Source Notes
129
Bibliography
134
For Further Reading
136
Index
139

If I had my time over I would do the same again. So would any man who dares to call himself a man.
—Nelson Mandela's statement before the judge who sentenced him to prison in 1962.

 # INTRODUCTION

"Our people demand democracy. Our country, which continues to bleed and suffer pain, needs democracy. It cries out for
the . . . freedom to speak of freedom. . . . We fight for . . . a future in which all shall—without regard to race, color, creed or
sex—have their right to vote."

The members of the United States Congress rose to their
feet and cheered as they heard Nelson Mandela speak these
words on June 26, 1990. Mandela was only the third foreign private citizen ever to address Congress. The others had been the
Marquis de Lafayette, the French nobleman who helped the
United States win the Revolutionary War, and Lech Walesa,
who had struggled to free Poland from Soviet domination.

Only months before, Mandela himself had gained his own
freedom. He had spent the past twenty-seven years in South
African jails, sent there for trying to win basic human rights for
the nonwhite people of South Africa.

Though he was now nearly seventy-two years old, Mandela had embarked on a world tour to gain support for the cause
in which he had spent his life. Everywhere he went, joyous
crowds turned out to see the man who had come to represent
the South African freedom struggle.

Mandela thanked Congress for its support in restricting trade and business with the white government of South Africa. He urged that these sanctions continue until the South African government took concrete steps to allow political rights for all of its people. The fight was still going on, and Mandela hoped to see victory before he died.

Yet he denied his own importance. He was not, he said, "a pretender to greatness." He was only "a particle of a people whom we know to be noble and heroic, enduring, multiplying, permanent, rejoicing in the expectation and knowledge that their humanity will be reaffirmed and enlarged."

Mandela ended his speech recalling the inspiration that he had taken from American heroes such as Jefferson, Washington, Lincoln, and Martin Luther King, Jr. Like Dr. King, he had a dream that would not die in the darkness of a prison cell: "The day may not be far when we will borrow the words of Thomas Jefferson and speak of the will of the South African nation: In the exercise of that will, by this united nation of black and white people, it must surely be that there will be born a country on the southern tip of Africa which you will be proud to call a friend and an ally because of its contribution to the universal striving towards liberty, human rights, prosperity, and peace among the people."

During his thirty-five-minute speech, Mandela was interrupted by applause nineteen times. Representative Ronald Dellums, chairman of the Congressional Black Caucus, enthusiastically called Mandela "a magnificent black man, a magnificent African." Tributes such as these came from all over the world.

Who is this man who aroused such pride and acclaim? How did he come to be an enduring symbol of the fight against racial injustice while spending much of his life in prison? What qualities enabled him to emerge after those long years with his spirit unbroken and without bitterness?

To discover the answers, we have to go back to his roots on the African farm where the life story of this extraordinary human being began.

1 "I LISTENED TO ELDERS OF OUR TRIBE"

Night comes to the Transkei with spectacular sunsets. In this place at the bottom of Africa, the grassland, or veld, grows in narrow strips between the Drakensberg Mountains and the Indian Ocean. The cone-shaped straw roofs of round huts, known as *rondavels,* stretch across the horizon. In the rolling fields of the *kraals,* or farms, men raise grain and tend cattle, both sources of wealth and prestige. Women husk corn and grind the kernels into mealie, the staple food. Trees dot the landscape.

For two thousand years, the Xhosa people, a group of related tribes who speak the Xhosa language, moved from central Africa to the Transkei. Each generation advanced the march south as new homesteads were established for the sons of the family. The Xhosas' long journey ended only when they approached the southern tip of the continent, the Cape of Good Hope.

During the nineteenth century, the Xhosa-speaking people clashed with a small number of Europeans who lived around the Cape. Through trickery and force of arms, the British took control of the Xhosas' land. They told the Xhosas where they could live, sometimes moving them to areas called reserves.

Into this world, Nelson Rolihlahla Mandela was born on July 18, 1918. His birthplace was a kraal near Umtata, capital of the Transkei reserve. The name Rolihlahla was prophetic. It means "stirring up trouble."

Nelson's family was a royal one. His great-great-grandfather was King Ngubengcuka, who had died more than one hundred years before. The king had ruled over the Thembu, one of several branches of the Xhosas, when their land belonged to them and they were free of European control. Nelson's father, Hendry Gadla, descended from a younger son of the king and so did not inherit great wealth or power. However, Hendry was a chief, and he owned enough cattle to have four wives. Nelson's mother was Nosekeni Fanny, Hendry's third wife.

Nelson, called Buti by his family, lived with his mother and three sisters in three whitewashed stone rondavels. One rondavel was used for cooking, one for sleeping, and the other for storing grain. While his sisters helped to grind corn into mealie, Buti learned the work done by other Xhosa boys. He helped plow the fields and herded cattle, sheep, and goats.

His parents were warm and affectionate. Nelson was close to his father's other eight children, who lived nearby in their mothers' homes. He was baptized into the Methodist Church and regularly attended services with his mother and sisters.

Nelson showed a keen desire for learning and was sent to a local school run by missionaries. The boy worked hard to learn reading, writing, and elementary arithmetic. His hunger for knowledge remained with him throughout his life.

When Nelson was ten, his father became ill. To make sure his son would continue his education, Hendry sent him to his relative, Jongintaba, the Paramount Chief of the Thembus. Hendry Mandela said, "I am giving you this servant, Rolihlahla. I can say from the way he speaks to his sisters and friends that his inclination is to help the nation. I want you to make him what you would like him to be. Give him education; he will follow your example." Nelson's father died soon after.

Nelson went to live in the Chief's Great Place in Mqekezweni. Years later, a relative recalled the arrival of the ten-year-old boy dressed in khaki shorts and shirt. "He was shy and, I think, lonely. So at first he didn't say much."

But the chief's wife became a second mother to him. She treated him with as much love as she showed her own son, named Justice. The two boys lived in their own rondavel with a younger brother of the Paramount Chief. They had only three beds, a table, and an oil lamp. At night, Nelson stayed up late studying the English and Xhosa languages as well as history and geography.

His new school, made up of a single room, had only two classes taught by three teachers.

After school, Nelson and the other boys changed into older clothes and went to herd the chief's cattle. In the pasture they also hunted small birds with their slingshots, roasting them over a fire. At night the boys milked the cows and brought the milk in pails to the family. Sometimes, the boys mounted the chief's horses and raced them—but "not very often," a relative remembers. For "Jongintaba was stern with us children as he was expected to be. He kept us at a distance, except when he needed to instruct us or reprimand us. He was very fair and just."

When Nelson was sixteen, he prepared for his circumcision ceremony, the official recognition that he had become a man. Accompanied by other young men of his age group, he went to the mountains, painted his face white, and wore a traditional grass skirt. There, tribal elders imparted the lore of the tribe and prepared the youths for the rites of manhood and for participation in the tribal councils.

Nelson was fascinated by the tribal courts, at which elders served as judges. The British-controlled central government allowed these courts to keep order in African areas. Nelson loved to listen to the judges question and cross-examine witnesses. Afterward, they came to a decision with the help of a tribal council. From this experience Nelson developed a respect for the law. But few could have guessed that he would one day become a lawyer in the great South African city of Johannesburg.

Nelson's traditional childhood insulated him from the condition of other black Africans in the country. He grew up with a sense of confidence and pride in himself and in his African heritage. He kept that pride throughout his life. He especially admired the Xhosas' strong idea of kinship. Whenever Xhosas traveled to another village or district, they could find a relative who would welcome them. If they were in need, they would even be given land and livestock to start a farm. That was the Xhosa way.

The Xhosa have a saying, "People are people through other people." This means that they see themselves as part of a group. Each individual gains power and a sense of identity from the group's unity. A person alone, without a group to belong to, is not really a person at all.

Nelson's sense of belonging to that group was reinforced by his experiences at the chief's kraal. Growing up, he loved to sit with the circle of people who gathered in the chief's rondavel at night. As the fire flickered, "I listened to elders of our tribe," he recalled. The elders told stories of the way life had been in Africa before the coming of the Europeans.

In those golden days, Nelson later wrote, "our people lived peacefully, under the democratic rule of their kings and Counsellors, and moved freely and confidently up and down the country. . . . We occupied the land, the forests, the rivers; we extracted the mineral wealth beneath the soil and all the riches of this beautiful country. We set up and operated our own government, we controlled our own armies and we organized our own trade and commerce."

But then the white settlers came, using rifles against the Xhosas' spears. The elders told how Nelson's ancestors fought to defend their homeland. Nelson was thrilled to hear about the bravery of the tribal warriors during those days of glory. But the stories always ended sadly, for the whites took the best part of the land for themselves. They had made some

14

of Nelson's ancestors sign papers, and then said that they had given up their right to the land. This was wrong, everyone knew, but the whites killed anyone who resisted them. The whites said that the laws of their courts proved that they now owned the land.

Nelson wondered about these pieces of paper and the white laws that seemed so different from what he had seen in the tribal courts. He became determined to devote his life to recovering the rights of his people. But first he would have to find out more about the land in which he lived and the white people who now ruled it.

THE SOURCES OF SOUTH AFRICAN CONFLICT

In 1910, eight years before Nelson's birth, the Union of South Africa was formed. This new country was made up of the British and Dutch territories of Southern Africa. The two groups of Europeans had long fought for control of the area, but the British had finally won.

The white history of South Africa began in 1652, when ships owned by the Dutch East India Company landed at the Cape of Good Hope. The Dutch wanted to establish a supply station for ships traveling from the Netherlands to the Dutch colonies in Asia. Dutch settlers soon followed, and they encountered the people already living in the Cape—the Khoi (Hottentots) and the San (Bushmen).

The Dutch leader, Jan van Riebeeck, built a hedge to keep the Africans out of his settlement. This hedge was the first of many dividing lines between the people of South Africa. From then to the present day, South Africa's history has been marked by the attempts to separate one people from another.

By the end of the seventeenth century, more Dutch and a sprinkling of French Huguenots (Protestants) and Germans had arrived at the Cape. The Dutch enslaved some Africans and brought Malay slaves from their colonies in the Dutch East Indies. Some Europeans married these Africans and Asians; their descendants were called Cape Coloreds. By the end of the eighteenth century, the Cape of Good Hope was a thriving colony.

In 1806, the British seized the colony from the Dutch, and soon British settlers added to the racial mix in South Africa. When slavery was abolished in the British Empire in 1834, the slaves in South Africa were freed. But to the Dutch farmers, or Boers, this meant an unacceptable change in their way of life.

In 1835, a great number of Boers set out on the Great Trek—a journey to the north and east, away from British influence. They traveled in small groups with their slaves, carrying their possessions and children in ox-drawn wagons. The Boers were a religious but tough people. Each wagon held both a Bible and a rifle. They believed they were fulfilling a divine destiny for their people. The Great Trek became the central event in the Boers' history. Their descendants, who call themselves Afrikaners, still celebrate the trek today.

To the Boers, a sign of God's blessing on their purpose came in 1838, when they encountered about twelve thousand Zulu warriors at the Ncome River in what is today's Natal Province. The Boers formed a *laager,* or circle, by drawing their ox wagons together. As the Zulus attacked with their spears, the Boers' rifles mowed them down. The river ran red with the blood of the slain, and today it is known as Blood River. A church stands there to commemorate the victory. And in today's South Africa, the date of the battle, December 16, is celebrated as the Day of the Covenant—the covenant between God and the Boers.

Yet the British, whose military power was greater than that of the Boers, soon followed them northward, extending British rule over Natal. The British built sugarcane plantations, and to work them brought a new element into South Africa's complicated mix of people. These were indentured laborers and free immigrants from India.

In response to the British expansion, the Boers moved farther inland, to the high veld, a grassy flatland plateau. The

Boers established new states; the two most important were the Orange Free State and the Transvaal. Here too the Boers subjugated the black population. The British recognized the independence of the Boer states in the 1850s, and for a short time the two European peoples coexisted in an uneasy peace.

Then, in 1867, diamonds were discovered north of the Cape Province, and the British absorbed the area into their colony. Nineteen years later, a large gold strike was made in the Transvaal. Land that had been thought useful only as farmland now became a rich prize. Prospectors poured in from all over the world. European capitalists bought land to develop the mineral resources. Kimberley, the chief town of the diamond region, and Johannesburg, the center of the gold-mining industry, mushroomed into major cities. Railroads were built inland from the Cape, bringing a new influx of foreigners. Mining operations increased the need for African laborers.

The Boers regarded these events as a threat to their way of life. They resented the *uitlanders* (outsiders) who now formed a growing part of the population. The Boers refused to grant political rights to these European immigrants. The tension between Boers and British led to the outbreak of the Boer War (1899–1902).

The British burned the Boers' farms to drive them off the land. When the Boer men formed commando groups to resist, the British rounded up their women and children and put them into camps in the south. For the first time, the world heard the term "concentration camps." Disease and famine raged in the camps, and thousands of Boers died of neglect and ill treatment.

The British triumphed in the Boer War, but the scars left by their victory lingered for generations. The Boers had been treated terribly; in response, they nursed their grievances and reinforced their strong feelings of nationality. Over the years, they had lost their sense of being Dutch—instead, they considered themselves "the white tribe of Africa." They began to refer to themselves as Afrikaners and to their language, a mixture of Dutch and African languages, as Afrikaans.

17

During the Boer War, the British had promised the African population that they would have the same rights as Europeans. But in the Treaty of Vereeniging that ended the war, the question of voting rights was postponed until the colony should be granted self-government.

In 1910, the African people were betrayed when the constitution for the Union of South Africa was written. The constitution restricted the right to vote to whites in all the provinces except the Cape. There, black Africans could vote for members of the new parliament. But no blacks were allowed to be members of the parliament.

When the proposed constitution became known, black South Africans sent a delegation to London to protest. But their arguments were ignored. Realizing that tribal divisions weakened their cause, a group of Africans formed the African National Congress (ANC) in 1912. Its purpose was to unite all the Africans in a single organization to represent their interests.

However, the new government of South Africa passed laws to further restrict Africans' rights. Blacks could own land only in the reserves that the British had established in the nineteenth century—such as the Transkei, where Nelson Mandela was born. And these reserves, by law, occupied less than 15 percent of the nation's territory.

Blacks could stay in European areas only as servants and laborers. Those who had carved out pieces of land as squatters or sharecroppers were evicted. Many African families were uprooted and forced onto the reserves. Solomon Plaatje, a black journalist, wrote, "The South African native found himself, not actually a slave, but a pariah [outcast] in the land of his birth."

But white South Africa still needed the labor of black Africans, particularly in the mines, where the hardest work was done by blacks. To control this labor force, a pass system (already in effect in British areas) was expanded throughout the country. Blacks could go outside the reserves, provided they carried passes proving that they were employed by a European. Clergymen and lawyers were exempt, but they still had to carry a certificate proving their occupation. No African could get a job or housing or be out after a curfew time without a pass. If an African was unable to show a pass on demand, he could be arrested and fined. The pass system turned every African outside his reserve into a potential criminal.

A WIDER WORLD

Nelson's school at Mqekezweni went only as high as the fifth grade. After he passed that level, Jongintaba drove him in the chief's automobile to a neighboring town that had a sixth grade in its school. When Nelson finished that year, the chief slaughtered a sheep for a feast of celebration. Nelson received a present of new leather shoes and a school uniform for high school. Nelson's graduation in 1938 was the occasion for another celebration. This time Jongintaba bought him a three-piece suit, for Nelson was bound for college.

In those days, young Africans living in the Cape Province still had an opportunity for higher education. Nelson enrolled at Fort Hare College, a Methodist school in eastern Cape Province. It was at Fort Hare that Nelson's political education began. Many of the college's teachers were active in politics. Also, many of the future South African leaders were among his classmates, though not all would take the same path that Nelson was to follow.

One of the most important friends Nelson made at Fort Hare was Oliver Tambo. Tambo had a wider experience of South African society than Nelson had. Tambo's father had been a farmer in Pondoland, another reserve, but Oliver attended high school in Johannesburg, the largest city in the country. There he did so well that he won a scholarship to Fort Hare. He and Nelson were to be lifelong friends and political allies.

Tambo recalls Nelson as being sensitive and quick to resent any slight but at the same time popular with other students. Another friend of Nelson's was Kaiser Matanzima, who told Nelson's biographer, "The two of us were very handsome young men and all the women wanted us."

Nelson and Matanzima enjoyed sneaking out of their dormitory at night to visit a local dance hall. Nelson learned the foxtrot and waltz, two popular Western-style dances of the day. However, the dance hall was definitely out of bounds for students. One night, Nelson asked a pretty young woman to dance. As they foxtrotted across the floor, Nelson learned her name. To his shock, she was the wife of a teacher, and Nelson spotted the teacher glaring at him from the other side of the room. He delivered the man's wife to him with sincere apologies. The teacher, "a very good sport," did not report Nelson's misbehavior.

But Nelson got into more serious trouble during his third year at the college. The students were unhappy with the food the college served, and the student council protested to the administration. In response, the school suspended the council's power. Nelson, who had been elected to the council, led a student strike. The administration suspended him for a year.

Nelson's feelings can be guessed as he went home to face Chief Jongintaba. The chief was upset by this disgrace and urged Nelson to cooperate with the school authorities when he was allowed to go back. But Nelson was never to return to Fort Hare.

For Jongintaba had another unpleasant surprise. As Nelson's guardian, he had decided it was time for Nelson to get married. He had even chosen a suitable wife, without bothering to consult Nelson. Preparations had gone too far for Nelson to object. The chief had already paid the bride's father *lobola,* the customary "bride-price."

Nelson's rebellious spirit flared up. As it happened, the chief's real son, Justice, Nelson's long-time friend, was also irked by his father's authority. Ignoring the chief's wedding arrangements for Nelson, the two young men decided to go to Johannesburg to seek their fortunes. They realized that they would need money, so they helped themselves to two of the chief's cattle and sold them.

20

Off they went, to the "Golden City" of the country, which both young men had long wanted to see. Nelson was leaving his old life behind. He gave up the chance to become a chief or a chief's counselor. He had other things on his mind, other plans for his life, but not even he could guess what lay ahead. The trip was the beginning of his long struggle to change his country.

2 A YOUNG MAN IN JOHANNESBURG

Nelson and Justice flagged down a bus on a country road and were off on the first leg of their journey. They left the bus at a train station and boarded a railroad car—one marked "non-Europeans only." They watched the scenery change as the train took them farther and farther from the Transkei. North through Natal, they saw the vast sugarcane plantations worked by laborers from India. Then they passed through the Drakensberg Mountains into the high veld of the Transvaal. Soon they could see the great mounds of earth that had been excavated from the gold mines. They were drawing near Egoli, "the city of gold," an African name for Johannesburg.

The two runaways were barely noticed, for they were among the thousands of South Africans who streamed into Johannesburg in 1941. "Jo-burg" had mushroomed in population since the mid-1930s. As new mines were opened, the city's economy boomed. The city's industries received a boost in 1939, when World War II broke out in Europe. South Africa's prime minister, Jan Christiaan Smuts, persuaded the nation's parliament to declare war on Germany—but the margin of votes was narrow, for many Boers opposed joining Britain's side in the war.

A booming economy was an opportunity for black Africans. They found it easy to get jobs in the country's steel and munition factories. They were also accepted as volunteers in the army but not in combat positions. They served as menial laborers, which was the role of blacks in all of South Africa's cities.

When Mandela arrived in 1941, Johannesburg was sharply divided along racial lines. The "Bantus" (the white term for all black Africans) lived in slum areas, known as townships, on the outskirts of the city. Ramshackle houses without electricity or sewage facilities were crowded next to each other in filthy, unpaved streets. Like Nelson and Justice, many of the Africans living in the townships had come from the countryside in search of work.

ARRIVAL

Nelson and Justice, of course, had no passes, no jobs, and no place to stay when they arrived in the city. Even if they had money to pay for a room, no hotel would admit blacks. But they did have an address: the office of the Crown Mines. Somehow they made their way through the huge city and found it. They knew that an overseer at the mines once had served at the court of Jongintaba. As their kinsman, he took them in and found jobs for them.

Mandela, tall and husky, was assigned to be a policeman. He stood guard at the entrance to the mine with a knobkerrie (a knobbed stick) and a whistle. The overseer promised that since Nelson could read and write, he might be promoted to clerk.

However, Jongintaba's reach was a long one. He soon found the man who had bought his stolen cattle and traced the boys to Johannesburg. The close-knit system of kinships worked as well for him as for the errant youths. Jongintaba sent a message to the overseer, and they lost their jobs. Justice returned to the Transkei, but Nelson persuaded Jongintaba to let him stay to continue his education.

Nelson must have found the city chaotic and bewildering.

Even so, he was fascinated by the high buildings, traffic jams, and crowds of people who passed through the streets on their way to and from work. He saw the full range of South Africa's population— Afrikaners, English and other Europeans, Indians, Cape Coloreds, and blacks of many tribes besides his own. It was very different from the sheltered life he had led in the Transkei with the privileges accorded to a member of the chief's family. Now Nelson had to make his own way in a tough urban society.

He survived by finding a Xhosa family who took him into their home in Alexandra township, north of the city. Then he needed a job. One of the neighbors advised him to get in touch with Walter Sisulu. Their meeting was to be a fateful one for the future of the black struggle.

Sisulu had been born in the Transkei six years before Mandela was born, but he had moved to Johannesburg in his late teens. He had taken the backbreaking job of "mine boy," hammering gold ore out of the earth deep underground. Later he began to write articles about Xhosa tribal heroes for a newspaper. When Nelson met him, Sisulu was running a small real estate agency for blacks looking for homes. He hired Nelson as an assistant.

Each day, Nelson commuted from Alexandra to his job in the city. His small salary had to pay for his food and rent, but he recalled that the family he stayed with didn't mind when he couldn't pay, and they served him a big meal each Sunday.

Some of Nelson's extra money was spent on dates with young women he met in Alexandra. An Anglican minister, also a Xhosa, advised him to date only Xhosa women. Nelson says he didn't take the advice, for at Fort Hare he had abandoned "thinking along ethnic lines."

However, as a "mampura," or country boy, Nelson had much to learn about city life. He once brought home a piece of meat he had purchased in the city. He asked the six-year-old daughter of the family to have her older sister cook it. The little girl smilingly told him that it was smoked meat—it didn't have to be cooked.

Nelson did not forget his dream of attaining a good education. He confided in Sisulu his ambition to become a lawyer. Sisulu lent Nelson the money to finish his college education through a correspondence course. When Nelson graduated from the University of South Africa in 1942, Sisulu bought him a suit and introduced him to the head of a white law firm. The law firm gave Nelson a clerk's job and sponsored his admission to the law school of the nearby University of Witwatersrand.

Working at the law firm brought Nelson his first social contact with whites. His new employers considered themselves enlightened people. The head typist had told him, "We have no color bar here. When the teaboy brings the tea, come and get yours from the tray." Two new teacups had been bought for Nelson and an Indian clerk, Gaur Radebe, to use. As Nelson recalled it, Radebe was an arrogant, "politically radical," little man. When the cups were passed around, Radebe told Nelson, "You watch and do exactly as I do." Radebe ignored his designated cup and took one of the old ones that the whites used. Embarrassed and shy, Nelson explained that he did not drink tea.

On another occasion, a white woman typist asked Nelson to give her some work. As he began dictating one of the papers he had to write, a white client walked into the office. The typist was embarrassed at being seen taking dictation from a black, and abruptly told Nelson to go to the drugstore and get her some shampoo. Nelson told the story with a smile. But he saw that all whites found it difficult to overcome the pervasive racism of South African society.

Nelson was ambitious and worked long hours. Even so, it was hard to carry out his duties at the firm while attending classes at the university and then returning home in time for the curfew that applied to blacks. One of the partners in the firm encouraged him to persevere. He told Nelson that by becoming a good lawyer he could earn "the respect of all sections of the population." However, the partner advised, he should avoid politics. It was one piece of advice Nelson did not take.

Despite the demands on his time and the ever-present shortage of money, Nelson fell in love. He met Evelyn Ntoko Mase at the home of Walter Sisulu's mother. The Sisulu household was a gathering place for Alexandra's young people, who talked politics and enjoyed each other's company. Evelyn was staying there temporarily. She too was from the Transkei. When her mother died, she came to Johannesburg to become a nurse.

There were many handsome young men at the Sisulus' parties, but Evelyn saw something "very special about Nelson." She fell in love the first time she saw him. The feeling was mutual, and Nelson, as usual, wasted no time after making up his mind. He soon made his marriage proposal through Evelyn's brother, as was the custom since her parents were dead. In 1944, Nelson and Evelyn registered their marriage at the Native Commissioners' Court in Johannesburg.

Evelyn wistfully recalled that they could not afford a wedding feast. Indeed, their biggest problem was finding a place to live. Apartments were scarce, for Alexandra was crowded with people who had come to work in Johannesburg's wartime industries.

Family ties again provided a solution. Evelyn's brother-in-law worked as a clerk for a mining company. He and his wife had a three-room house for themselves and their two children. They offered the newlyweds one of the rooms free of charge.

A GROWING POLITICAL CONSCIOUSNESS

Oliver Tambo, Nelson's friend from Fort Hare College, soon appeared in Walter Sisulu's circle of friends. He had come to the city to look for a job as a teacher. Sisulu brought both Nelson and Tambo to a meeting of the African National Congress. Sisulu had joined the ANC in 1940, and Nelson and Tambo signed up as members in 1944.

By the time Nelson Mandela joined the ANC, the organization's early vigor had faded. The group had sent petitions to the South African government and staged passive-resistance demonstrations. But the government responded with laws creating even greater discrimination. In 1936, black Africans lost their right to vote for white representatives in the national parliament. Many blacks regarded the organization as ineffective and irrelevant.

Along with other young Africans, Mandela, Sisulu, and Tambo set out to revitalize the ANC. The young reformers were determined to change it from a "body of gentlemen with clean hands" to an organization that would more effectively oppose the policies of the South African government. Rather than challenge the older leaders directly, they formed a Youth League within the ANC.

In one statement of their philosophy, the young reformers declared: "The Congress Youth League must be the brainstrust and power-station of the spirit of African nationalism; the spirit of African self-determination; the spirit that is so discernible in the thinking of our youth. It must be an organization where young African men and women will meet and exchange ideas in an atmosphere pervaded by a common hatred of oppression." The Youth League's leaders stressed the positive values of African culture more than the early ANC leaders had.

The ANC's membership consisted of the country's best-educated blacks, but the Youth League intended to reach the great majority of the African people. World War II stimulated the Youth League's organizing efforts. The war against the racist Nazi regime abroad encouraged the desire for freedom at home. The year 1940 was the first year in the country's history that parliament passed no new laws restricting the freedoms of racial groups.

Although the South African government forbade Africans to strike, several strikes occurred during the war. In another action, the people of Alexandra boycotted the bus service to protest a rise in the fare. Even though it was midwinter, Mandela, his wife, and thousands of others chose to walk to work rather than pay. After nine days, the bus fare was reduced.

In 1945, after the Allied victory in World War II, the ANC took part in the victory march in Johannesburg. It was the biggest parade the city had ever seen. Twenty thousand black Africans followed a marching band, waving the ANC flag bearing the colors black (for the people), green (for the land), and gold (for the wealth of their country). Their slogan was "Let's finish the job!"

THE GENERAL SECRETARY

In 1946, the rights' struggle in South Africa shifted to the Indian population. Most Indians were descended from those who had come to work on the sugar plantations in Natal in the nineteenth century. Though many Indians had prospered—some owned shops and businesses—they, like the blacks and Cape Coloreds, were relegated to second-class status by South African law.

Earlier in the century, Mohandas ("Mahatma") Gandhi, then a young Indian lawyer in South Africa, had organized his first "passive resistance" campaign to protest the South African government's mistreatment of Indians. Later, Gandhi would employ this same technique to win independence for India from Great Britain.

After World War II, the South African government decided to segregate the Indian population in certain areas, much as blacks were. The Indians organized protest demonstrations. One of the leaders of the movement was Ismail Meer, a fellow law student of Nelson's at the University of Witwatersrand. The two had become friends, and Nelson frequently stayed at Ismail's apartment when he could not make the long trip home after class.

Mandela was impressed by the Indians' dedication and hard work. Attending the planning sessions over curry and tea in Ismail's apartment was an exhilarating experience for him. It was the first time he had seen how to organize a successful protest against the government.

Taking law classes at Witwatersrand also opened Nelson's eyes to the fact that many groups in South Africa opposed the government's racist policies. Besides Indian students, he also

28

met whites who wanted to change their nation. Among them were Communists such as Joe Slovo and Bram Fischer.

An ugly incident on a public bus showed Nelson that his new friends were ready to fight for their rights—and sometimes win. Nelson and three Indian students, including Ismail Meer, boarded the bus without thinking anyone would mind them traveling together. But the conductor, an Afrikaner, suddenly confronted them. He seemed more angry at the Indians, telling them they were not allowed to ride with a "kaffir."

Kaffir was an Afrikaner term that roughly corresponds to "nigger." The Indian students began to berate the conductor for using such a crude word. Finally, the conductor stopped the bus and called a policeman. The officer arrested the Indians and told Mandela to come along as a witness. At the police station, Nelson refused to give a statement against his friends, and he too was charged.

The next day they went to court, with Bram Fischer as their lawyer. When the case was called, the judge greeted Fischer warmly. It turned out that the judge and Fischer's father—another judge—were old friends. The charges were swiftly dismissed.

Fischer and other white friends invited Nelson to join the South African Communist Party (SACP). Nelson was flattered. The SACP was the only political party willing to accept black Africans, and it had drawn support from some African nationalists. But Nelson rejected communism because of his strong Christianity.

At this time, Nelson was wary of any outside influence on the black African movement. He remained convinced that Africans must develop their own leaders and create strategies for winning their rights on their own. They might learn from others, but they could not allow others to lead them.

In 1946, black African mine workers organized a strike. Seven of Johannesburg's mines were shut down; an estimated seventy thousand workers joined the strike. It was a serious threat to the economy of a country so dependent on its gold and diamond mines. The government responded by sealing off the workers' living quarters. Then police with rifles and batons forced the men back to work. Some workers were killed, and the strike was broken.

The violent reaction of the government revealed to Mandela one of the weaknesses of the white-dominated society. Because the bulk of the work force was black, the nation was vulnerable to united black protest. However, the great fear of the whites was that allowing blacks full voting rights would mean a black government that would expel Europeans. Whites would take any steps to prevent that.

The following year Mandela became general secretary of the ANC Youth League. Receiving this post was a sign that others had begun to notice his leadership abilities. A policy statement issued by the Youth League addressed the issue of white fears of a black-dominated society: "We realize that the different racial groups have come to stay. But we insist that a condition of interracial peace and progress is the abandonment of white domination. . . . Therefore, our goal is the winning of national freedom for African people, and the inauguration of a people's free society where racial oppression and persecution will be outlawed."

Nelson had new family responsibilities as well. Evelyn had given birth to a son they named Thembi. As a family, they were finally able to move into a home of their own in Soweto (short for Southwest Township), outside Johannesburg. Though their "match-box house" had only three rooms, the Mandelas freely offered their hospitality to others—just as they had earlier received it. Nelson's younger sister Leabie came to stay, and Nelson enrolled her in a local high school. Evelyn gave birth to a second child, a daughter, but she was a frail baby and died within a year.

In 1949, Nelson's mother Fanny became ill in the Transkei. He had her brought to Johannesburg for medical treatment, and she too moved in with them. Evelyn considered that a blessing, for her presence made the household seem more like the extended families they had known in the Transkei. Friends often dropped by, and visitors from the Transkei knew that the Mandelas would always take them in, even if some had to sleep on the floor.

When Fanny recovered, she helped with the housework and cared for Thembi during the day. This was very welcome help, for both Nelson and Evelyn worked long hours. Evelyn had now found a job as a nurse, and her wages provided most of the family's income. She too became politically active, joining a nurses' union to win better pay for black nurses, who received much less than whites.

Nelson was still attending law classes, and his work for the ANC sometimes took him away for several days at a time. He was carrying out the Youth League's plan to win support among all classes of blacks. He and others visited townships in the Transvaal, organizing new chapters of the Youth League.

To keep up with all his duties, Nelson had to be a highly organized person. He rose at dawn and jogged before breakfast. He also took up boxing as another way of keeping physically fit. However, according to Evelyn, he was by no means a macho male. He shopped for the family's food, enjoyed bathing the babies, and took over the cooking chores when everyone else was busy.

His energy constantly found new outlets. He joined the International Club, a multiracial group that brought whites and blacks together for social evenings. Some blacks were bitter toward all whites, but that was never Nelson's way.

It was a happy time for the Mandelas. Though poor, they had enough for themselves and for visitors as well. They were all working for the great goal of black rights, and the future seemed bright. Neither Nelson nor Evelyn could foresee the hardships that they would soon face.

3 "NO EASY WALK TO FREEDOM"

In other parts of Africa, black independence movements blossomed after World War II. All were destined to succeed. Today, white minority rule remains only in South Africa. In fact, that rule actually became harsher when the Afrikaner Nationalist party (ANP) came to power in 1948.

Under the leadership of Prime Minister Daniel Malan, this party was committed to *apartheid,* the "apartness" of the races. The ultimate goal of apartheid was to maintain white supremacy by completely separating all of South Africa's racial groups—black from white, black from colored, and colored from Indian and black, but also Xhosas from Zulus and other blacks, and even Afrikaans-speaking whites from English-speaking whites. Each group was to live in assigned areas where it could "develop along its own lines." The word *apartheid* became a worldwide synonym for racism and injustice.

Beginning in 1948, the Afrikaner government passed new laws that strengthened the discriminatory system already in place. In 1950, the Population Registration Act classified the country's population into four major categories: Europeans, Asians, Coloreds, and Bantus (black South Africans). It created a population register to fix the racial category of every person in the country. By the Group Areas Act, the towns and rural areas were divided into zones in which only one race could live, own property, and conduct business. Not surprisingly, the most desirable areas were set aside for whites.

The Bantu Education Act of 1953 was an important part of the apartheid program. This law did away with most academic subjects in black schools and substituted training in such activities as tree planting. Blacks were to be educated for menial work only. Schooling for black children was reduced to three hours a day. The government closed the mission schools that had formerly educated blacks and coloreds, and all non-whites were now excluded from the established universities.

Local laws created segregation in all areas where it formerly did not apply. Segregation was extended to buses, trains, movie theaters, and post offices.

It was not possible to bar all blacks from white areas, for, as Mandela had seen, white society still needed black workers in mines and industry, and as servants. Thus, blacks with passes could still enter the cities, but they had to live in the "townships" on the outskirts of the cities. Apartheid law required women to carry passes as well; formerly only men had to.

Blacks not needed for labor were relegated to "homelands," based on the boundary lines of the old reserves. These homelands occupied 13 percent of the total area of the country, even though black Africans made up about 70 percent of South Africa's population. Typically, a man who held a job in the city was not able to obtain permission for his wife and children to live in the township with him. They had to remain in a distant "homeland."

The chief difference between the homelands and the old reserves was that the government planned to make the homelands independent. Thus, their residents would have a separate citizenship and no claim to civil rights in South Africa.

All forms of protest against the government were limited by the passage of the Suppression of Communism Act of 1950. Under the guise of fighting communism, the government made illegal virtually any form of written or spoken opposition to the government. Newspapers were censored, books were banned, and many political meetings were outlawed.

DEVISING A NEW STRATEGY

Mandela and his friends naturally were alarmed by the new political situation. In 1949, the leaders of the Youth League confronted the leadership of the ANC and demanded a greater voice in the organization. Walter Sisulu was appointed secretary-general of the ANC, and Mandela became a member of its national executive board.

The ANC adopted a more militant program. It denounced apartheid and called for an end to white domination. But as Mandela said, the group's emphasis would change from "pleading their cause" to bringing pressure "to compel the authorities to grant their demands." In its new Program of Action, the ANC announced its intention to use mass actions such as boycotts, strikes, and civil disobedience.

As a start, the ANC decided to call a one-day work stoppage by blacks on May 1, 1950. But before the planning got off the ground, another group announced its own protest—a public demonstration in Johannesburg—for the same day. Mandela and his associates were furious at what they saw as an attempt to divide the movement. The organizers of the rival protest were members of the Transvaal branch of the ANC, the Communist party, and the Indian National Congress. Mandela still felt that Africans should go it alone in their actions. He and his associates strongly criticized the rival organizers.

However, the Johannesburg protest went on anyway. Mandela and Sisulu were there and saw that it was a success. Over half of the workers stayed home. However, the day ended tragically as police attacked crowds of black demonstrators, killing eighteen people and wounding more than thirty.

The May Day protest caused a change in Mandela's thinking. He called it "a turning point in my life." Not only was it the first time he had seen police violence firsthand, but he saw that black African workers were ready to give their support to a mass movement that included nonblacks. From then on, Mandela would willingly work with nonblack groups in a common struggle.

Thus, the ANC now joined forces with the South African Communist party and the Indian National Congress. The groups announced a national work stoppage of all nonwhite groups for June 26, 1950. This was the first time the ANC publicly backed such a large, multiracial demonstration. Mandela worked tirelessly, traveling around the Transvaal, speaking to groups, trying to win support for the work stoppage. All the time, he worried about his wife Evelyn, who was in the last month of her third pregnancy. And when she gave birth to a son, Makgatho, Mandela was with her.

The June 26 work stoppage was a limited success. In Durban and other small cities, almost all the workers stayed home. Partial work stoppages took place in Johannesburg and Cape Town. However, the farm workers in the Transvaal, which had been the responsibility of the ANC, failed to respond in great numbers.

Nevertheless, Mandela gained experience and a national reputation. At the end of the year he was elected president of the ANC Youth League. His personal qualities drew the respect and admiration of all who met him. He had a keen sense of humor, an interest in other people, a determination not to become discouraged, and devotion to his friends.

Oliver Tambo summed up what others felt about Mandela: "He has the natural air of authority. He cannot help magnetizing a crowd: he is commanding, with a tall handsome bearing; trusts and is trusted by the youth, for their impatience reflects his own; appealing to the women. He is dedicated and fearless. He is the born mass leader."

In working with the Indian National Congress, Mandela became more interested in the techniques of passive resistance that Mohandas Gandhi had used to win the independence of India. He agreed with Walter Sisulu that the ANC's next stage of protest should be a campaign of civil disobedience, like Gandhi's.

35

VOLUNTEER-IN-CHIEF

Though Gandhi had shown that nonviolent protest could work, Mandela and his colleagues worried that it would be difficult to persuade others to use it. Imagine yourself as a black South African, exposed to insults and indignities in every aspect of daily life. When you try to protest, police use dogs, clubs, and guns against you and your family. Could you remain nonviolent under such conditions? The only way such a movement could succeed would be through the intense discipline and self-control of its members. The ANC leaders wondered if they could persuade others to follow them in such a movement.

Nonetheless, they decided to try. In December 1951, the ANC approved the beginning of mass protests on April 6 of the following year. That same day, white South Africans would be celebrating the three-hundredth anniversary of the founding of the Cape Colony. The ANC demonstration would demand repeal of the unjust laws and declare that those laws would be defied peacefully if they were not repealed.

Mandela was placed in charge of the Defiance Campaign of 1952 as "volunteer-in-chief." Risking arrest, he traveled throughout the country to explain the plan to groups of people. Sometimes alone, sometimes with Tambo as a companion, he often arrived at night. In the townships, there were no taxis or telephones. He had to walk miles from a train or bus station, and find an unfamiliar house where someone would take him in. He could not count on finding a distant Xhosa kinsman, and Africans often distrusted strangers who were not of their tribal group. Mandela's only appeal was that he was black and so were they. Even so, he and Tambo were often turned away by someone who feared police reprisals.

The government's attitude was made clear when the ANC wrote a letter to Prime Minister Malan announcing its planned demonstration. The letter set forth Africans' grievances, saying that government repression was now "a matter of life and death." The prime minister's secretary wrote a reply that said Africans should send their messages to the Minister of Native

Affairs. The secretary said that there was no sense arguing that "Bantus" were no different from Europeans, since the clear differences between them "are permanent and not man-made." The government's apartheid laws were intended to be "protective."

So, on April 6, thousands of black Africans turned out for the beginning of the Defiance Campaign. All over the country people assembled to pray for freedom and to hear speakers ask for volunteers to defy the apartheid laws. Mandela spoke to a crowd in a union hall in Johannesburg. He warned them that the government response to volunteers would be harsh. But they must not return force with violence. The protesters must keep the dignity that would bring success for their cause.

In the days that followed, Mandela continued to travel to sign up more volunteers. When he visited Cape Town, his appearance caused a sensation. Blacks in white areas generally walked head down, showing proper "respect." Mandela, the tall and stately chief's son, strode along the sidewalks as though the city were already his. A white man who saw him said, "I noticed people turning and staring . . . and I saw this magnificent figure of a man, immaculately dressed. Not just blacks but whites, including white women, were turning to admire him."

On his trips as volunteer-in-chief, Mandela met Chief Albert Luthuli, who was soon to become president of the ANC. In his youth, Luthuli had not been a radical. He had taught literature in a high school for fifteen years before the members of his Zulu tribe chose him as chief. Luthuli's people lived on the Groutville reserve in Natal. Like Mandela's foster-father, Jongintaba, he had judged disputes between his people and served the national government by keeping the peace. A devout Christian, he had traveled to the United States and other countries to attend conferences of Christian missionaries.

In 1946, Luthuli accepted a post on the Native Representative Council, the only South African government body that blacks could serve on. But that same year, the council disbanded to protest its lack of real power, and Luthuli joined the ANC.

He had decided that cooperation with the government brought no results.

Like many other Africans, Luthuli felt that the Defiance Campaign offered a new hope. Beginning on June 26, 1952, people began to defy the apartheid laws in whatever way they could. Some marched through "Europeans Only" entrances to train stations or post offices. Others stayed out after curfew or refused to carry their passes. Indians entered black townships. The police hauled thousands of people to jail.

Mandela had warned the volunteers not to retaliate, no matter what the provocation. His own self-control was tested on the first day of the campaign, when he addressed a meeting in Johannesburg after the curfew hour of 11 P.M. He was arrested, along with many of those present, and calmly entered the police van.

But it was harder to keep his temper when someone else was the target of violence. When the prisoners reached the jail, a policeman shoved one of Mandela's companions down a flight of stairs. When Mandela stepped forward to help the man, the police kicked him aside. Mandela demanded that the man be given medical attention but was ignored. All night long, Mandela lay in his cell listening to the groans of the injured man down the corridor. Nonviolence was indeed a difficult path to follow.

Mandela was soon released on bail, and continued organizing others to go on with the campaign. The police had arrested thousands of people but now decided to target the leaders. On July 30, police raided homes and offices, seizing papers and arresting Mandela, Sisulu, and around thirty others. The charge brought against them was violating the Suppression of Communism Act. The arrests spurred new demonstrations, but some of them became violent in the absence of experienced leaders. By November, the ANC decided to temporarily end the campaign.

Only around 8,500 people had actually broken laws, but the influence of the Defiance Campaign was greater than the number of people who participated. Many thousands of blacks became aware that it *was* possible to resist apartheid. Membership in the ANC soared. In repressing the campaign, the government had aroused the sympathy to the cause even among whites. At the trial in November, the judge noted that Mandela and the other leaders had advised demonstrators to remain peaceful. He gave them suspended sentences on condition they did not repeat the crime.

The government noted the role that Albert Luthuli had played in the campaign. He was ordered to resign from the ANC. When he refused, the government stripped him of his office as chief of his Zulu people. The action was intended to shame him, and indeed Luthuli, twenty years older than Mandela, must have regretted the loss of his peaceful life as an honored chief in a rural homeland. But he wrote, "Who will deny that thirty years of my life have been spent knocking in vain, patiently, moderately, and modestly at a closed and barred door? . . . I have joined my people in the new spirit that moves them today, [that] expresses itself in a determined and non-violent manner."

A month later, in December 1952, the ANC elected Luthuli as its new president. Nelson was named to be his deputy, a recognition of the role he had played in the Defiance Campaign. Both men, now in the forefront of the freedom movement, became special targets of the government. It issued "banning" orders against Luthuli and Mandela, along with other leaders of the ANC, the Indian Congress, and the labor unions.

BANNED

Banning was one of the chief weapons that the South African government used against opponents of its policies. A ban was a government order that restricted the conduct and travel of the banned person. Organizations could also be banned, making it illegal for them to operate in any way. But the government was not ready to take that step against the ANC. Instead, it hoped to cripple the ANC by banning its leaders.

The ban order on Mandela required him to remain in Johannesburg (including the townships) and prohibited him from attending public meetings. It was to last six months, but a few months after it expired, it was renewed for two years.

When the ANC elected new leaders, they too were banned. Seeing that the government's actions would hinder mass demonstrations, Mandela realized that new political strategies were necessary. He proposed working harder to organize blacks in the townships. In what became known as the M Plan (M for Mandela), the ANC began to organize people on a block-by-block basis. This would enable the ANC to build greater mass support and would involve greater numbers in the organization. It also made it harder to destroy the organization, since it would not be as dependent on a few leaders.

The M Plan was announced in a speech that Mandela wrote to be delivered to the Transvaal ANC in 1953. Earlier in the year he had been elected president of that branch, but because he was banned, he could not attend the meeting in person. Yet his words stirred the group.

He asked all the members "to redouble their efforts. . . . The hard and strenuous task of recruiting members and strengthening our organization through a house-by-house campaign . . . must be done by you all."

Mandela concluded his speech: "You can see that there is no easy walk to freedom anywhere, and many of us will have to pass through the valley of the shadow of death again and again before we reach the mountain tops of our desires. Dangers and difficulties have not deterred us in the past, they will not frighten us now. But we must be prepared for them. . . . [We must make the ANC] the bright and shining instrument that will cleave its way to Africa's freedom."

Somehow, during all this political activity, Mandela finished his law studies in 1952. He and Oliver Tambo set up a law office in Johannesburg. They rented the space from a sympathetic Indian merchant. Most of their clients were victims of the apartheid laws.

As Tambo later wrote, "South African apartheid laws turn

innumerable innocent people into 'criminals.'" People were arrested on such petty charges as violating curfew, having an expired pass, being in a white or colored or Indian area without permission, or simply being "cheeky" (disrespectful) toward a white person. Mandela and Tambo defended many young people who had taken out their rage against the apartheid system by committing vandalism or petty theft. Tambo said that if he and Mandela had not opposed apartheid when they began their law practice, their experiences would soon have turned them into rebels. "Every case in court, every visit to the prison to interview clients, reminded us of the humiliation and suffering burning into our people."

Some judges and prosecutors treated them courteously, but others were openly hostile. Mandela refused to play the humble role expected of blacks. He could be devastating and sarcastic when questioning white policemen and objecting to judges' rulings. Because of Mandela's leadership of the Defiance Campaign, the Transvaal Law Society tried to have him disbarred, but the Supreme Court ruled in his favor.

At all times, Mandela defended his clients vigorously. One of his clients was a black servant accused of stealing several articles of clothing from the woman who employed her. The clothing was produced as evidence. Mandela called the white employer to the stand and picked a pair of panties from the pile of clothing. "Are these yours?" he asked the woman. The employer flushed, too embarrassed to discuss her underwear with a black man. She replied, "No," and the judge had to dismiss the case.

THE FREEDOM CHARTER

In 1953, a former teacher at Fort Hare College, Dr. Z. K. Matthews, proposed a new Congress of the People. It would bring together sympathetic groups from all races to draw up a Freedom Charter outlining their goals for a democratic, multiracial South Africa.

Two years later the plan came to fruition. The ANC, along with Indian, colored, and white organizations, formed a Congress Alliance. Representatives from each group met to write the Freedom Charter. They came with letters from all parts of the country, written by ordinary people who had responded to circulars that posed the question: "IF YOU COULD MAKE THE LAWS ... WHAT WOULD YOU DO? HOW WOULD YOU SET ABOUT MAKING SOUTH AFRICA A HAPPY PLACE FOR ALL THE PEOPLE WHO LIVE IN IT?"

On June 25, 1955, almost three thousand delegates to the Congress assembled in a field at Kliptown, southwest of Johannesburg. One of them later described the throng, many of whom were wearing the ANC colors of gold, black, and green:

> *Large African grandmothers, wearing Congress skirts, Congress blouses or Congress cloths on their heads, traipsing around with baggy suitcases; young Indian housewives, with glistening saris and shawls embroidered with Congress colors; gray old African men, with walking sticks and Congress arm bands; young city workers from Johannesburg, with broad hats, bright American ties and narrow trousers; smooth Indian lawyers and businessmen, moving confidently among the crowd in well-cut suits.*

Nelson was present, although his ban forbade him from attending large gatherings. At first he watched from a nearby house, but he could not restrain his joy, and on the second day of the gathering he put on a disguise and mingled with the crowd. A disguise was necessary because the police were there too, taking photographs. The government regarded this peaceful gathering as a grave threat.

For two days, the Congress went smoothly. The delegates cheered the reading of the Freedom Charter, which began, "We the people of South Africa declare for all our country and the world to know: that South Africa belongs to all who live in it, black and white, and that no government can justly claim authority unless it is based on the will of all the people." The charter urged a "one person, one vote" policy as the only means of attaining this goal. It also called for an equitable sharing of the country's wealth.

The government regarded this as treason. On the afternoon of the third day of the meeting, the police moved in. A policeman took the microphone on the speaker's platform and announced that police forces had surrounded the field. No one could leave until he or she had been questioned and searched.

The interrogations dragged on long into the night. Police set up lights and checked the passes of blacks, Indians, and coloreds. They photographed the white delegates. Any papers a person carried were placed into envelopes and carefully labeled. At some point, someone began to sing, and the crowd took it up until the ordeal was over.

Sadly, however, controversy over the Freedom Charter soon split the ANC into two groups. Even though the Congress meeting had begun with a special award honoring Albert Luthuli, he took offense at the fact that he had not been shown the charter before it was read to the delegates. He had been ill at the time. Though Mandela and Sisulu had approved the final draft of the document, there had been too little time to show it to all of the ANC's leaders.

At the ANC's annual meeting, others rose to attack the charter. Its chief opponents were "Africanists," who still felt suspicious that white and Indian groups were trying to use the black movement for their own ends. Others felt that the charter showed too much Communist influence; some claimed it had been mostly written by whites.

Mandela, Sisulu, and others led the "Chartists," who urged the ANC to officially approve the Freedom Charter. After heated discussion, a majority of the leadership agreed. But the rift between the Africanists and Chartists was not healed; it would soon break out again.

Mandela was often away from home on political work. And the Mandelas' marriage felt the strain. Evelyn enrolled in a special nurses' course to become a midwife. She lived in the nursing school in Durban. Mandela visited her only when his duties took him to that part of the country. Back in Soweto, Mandela's mother and sisters took care of the couple's two young sons, Thembi and Makgatho.

When Evelyn finished her course, she moved back to their home in Soweto. Nelson's ban kept him in the area, and Evelyn secretly felt it was a blessing in disguise. Now they could be together as a family again.

Nelson was always a loving father. He told his sons the stories he himself had heard in the chief's rondavel in the Transkei. He explained to them how the trouble began between whites and blacks. Sometimes he took them to meetings of an ANC youth group in Soweto, to boxing tournaments, or to the movies. Wherever they went, people recognized Nelson and called out to him. The boys were proud that their father was such a great man, with so many friends.

Mandela could be strict too. One day, his younger son Makgatho asked Nelson for money to go to the local swimming pool. When Nelson asked how much it cost to get in, Makgatho told him double the real price. Nelson knew Makgatho was lying, but he gave him the money. However, he followed Makgatho and saw him give half of the money to a friend. Nelson called Makgatho over and asked why he had lied. Makgatho felt so ashamed he couldn't speak. But Nelson kept asking until Makgatho confessed that his friend didn't have any money, and so he had asked for the price of two admissions. Nelson said it was good to be concerned about his friend, but why did he lie about it? Makgatho said he was afraid, and Nelson told him never to be afraid of telling the truth.

In 1953, Evelyn became pregnant again and later gave birth to a daughter, named Maki. Evelyn's joy was short-lived. During her pregnancy she began to hear rumors that Nelson was seeing another woman. When she confronted him, he became angry and moved his bed into another room. Evelyn asked others what she should do. She went to Walter Sisulu for help, but Nelson was further offended when he heard that she had taken their troubles outside the home.

The family, including Nelson's sisters and mother, all felt the strain. Leabie, Nelson's younger sister, recalled that "the two people we respected, [were] suddenly turning on each other . . . it was as if the ground below us was breaking and we were falling."

Evelyn felt the same way. She later said, "He was the only man I ever loved. He was a wonderful husband and a wonderful father." But things went from bad to worse. They began to quarrel over the way he treated Thembi, their older son. Evelyn thought he was too generous about giving money to Thembi. It was a small dispute, but it brought to a head all the troubles between them. Nelson moved out and filed for divorce. Evelyn did not contest it, and the marriage of twelve years ended.

4 THE TREASON TRIAL

A government that fears its own people maintains control by creating even greater fear. South Africa's government responded to the Freedom Charter by staging police raids in the middle of the night. On December 5, 1956, Nelson was awakened by loud knocking at the door of the house he shared with his mother and sisters. The police pawed through the few possessions the Mandelas owned, looking for evidence. Then Nelson was thrust into a police van and taken away.

All over South Africa the police rounded up blacks, Indians, coloreds, and whites, searching offices as well as homes in an action code-named Operation T. In all, 156 persons were arrested and flown in government helicopters to the Fort, as the prison in Johannesburg was known. Among those arrested were Oliver Tambo, Albert Luthuli, and Walter Sisulu.

The government charged the prisoners with high treason. It accused them of being part of a Communist-inspired conspiracy to overthrow the South African government by force.

PREPARING FOR A LONG TRIAL
On December 19, 1956, the preparatory examination of the Treason Trial opened. Early that morning, crowds had gath-

ered in the streets around the courthouse carrying signs reading: "We Stand By Our Leaders." They sang the anthem of the ANC and other ballads of freedom. The following day even more people showed up, and police fired rifles at them to drive them away. Twenty-two people were wounded.

The prisoners were brought into the courtroom and locked in a huge cage with a sign that read "DON'T FEED," as if they were animals. The defense lawyers pointed to this as an example of government brutality. The judge agreed and allowed them to be released on bail.

No hotels in Johannesburg would admit any nonwhites. Nelson opened his house to as many as he could, and lodgings were found for the rest. The government had brought to one place virtually all the leaders of South Africa's human rights movement, many of whom had never met before. Now they could freely exchange ideas and plans.

The prosecution narrowed in on the policy of the ANC from 1952 to 1956. The Freedom Charter was regarded as the crucial piece of evidence. The prosecution also accused the ANC of instigating violence during the Defiance Campaign of 1952. Thousands of documents, including Mandela's speeches and published articles, were introduced as evidence. Among the incriminating documents were two signs that had been placed over food stalls in the field where the Freedom Charter was first read aloud. These suspicious signs read, "Soup with Meat" and "Soup without Meat."

During this first phase of the trial, Albert Luthuli called for all citizens to stay at home for one day to protest apartheid and to demonstrate the need for a living wage. As Mandela explained, the call for citizens to stay at home, rather than invite violence by picketing, was to show the nonviolent character of the movement. The "stay at home" action was particularly effective in Johannesburg and in Port Elizabeth, the center of the automobile industry on the Indian Ocean.

The preliminary stage lasted until September 1957, when the court decided that there was enough evidence to hold a trial. Until the start of the trial, the defendants were free to go to their homes. During this recess, the charges of high treason were withdrawn for Luthuli, Oliver Tambo, and many other defendants. But Mandela was not one of them.

COURTING WINNIE

During the Treason Trial, Nelson met Winnie Madikizela. Their meeting would lead to a political partnership that would have a long-term effect on South Africa.

Nomzamo Winnie Madikizela was born in 1936 in the Pondoland region of the Transkei. Nomzamo means "she who strives" in Xhosa, and "Winnie" was added to her name at her baptism as a Methodist. She was the daughter of Columbus and Gertrude Madikizela. One of nine children, Winnie grew up in an extended family that often included twenty or thirty homeless children whom the family had taken in.

Both Columbus and Gertrude were teachers, but their salaries did not go far with so many children to support. Winnie recalled, "I became aware at an early stage that the whites felt superior to us. And I could see how shabby my father looked in comparison to the white teachers. That hurts your pride when you are a child."

Winnie's mother was fanatically religious, and often locked Winnie and her younger sister in a room, forcing them to pray aloud for hours. When one of Winnie's older sisters was stricken with tuberculosis, all her mother's prayers could not save her. After the sister died, Winnie's mother's spirit was broken, and she seemed to be wasting away. Winnie recalled watching her lie in her bed, growing weaker each day. "She was literally disappearing, and she was in great pain; that's all I remember," Winnie wrote years later. No doctor in that part of the country could treat such an illness.

Winnie channeled her anger and sorrow into a fierce determination to excel. She completed all of the courses in her village school and went away to attend a Methodist high school in the town of Shawbury. Like Nelson, Winnie was shy at first, but her inexhaustible energy soon won her friends, and her confidence rose. She excelled at sports, joined the debate club, and kept her grades high.

After graduation, Winnie was accepted at the Jan Hofmeyr School of Social Work in Johannesburg. This was a wonderful opportunity because the school was the only one in South Africa where blacks could receive a degree in social work.

Johannesburg was as thrilling for Winnie as it had been for Nelson. She too had never been out of the Transkei before. Blacks in Johannesburg had their own newspaper and magazines. One of them printed her photograph, for she was not only a star student but also strikingly beautiful.

Politics was the everyday topic at the lunch table and in the dormitory where Winnie lived. Many of the other black students were members of the ANC. They distributed copies of the Freedom Charter. But Winnie concentrated on her studies, and in due course she received her diploma with honors.

Soon Winnie was faced with a decision. She had been awarded a scholarship to continue her studies at a college in the United States. Naturally, she was overjoyed. With time, she could prepare herself to return to South Africa and truly help her people.

A few days later, however, Winnie received a letter from the Baragwanath Hospital. She had visited and lectured at the hospital, and the officials had been impressed. They offered her a job as a social worker. This too was an honor, for if she accepted, she would be the first black to hold such a position in South Africa.

Winnie agonized over the decision. The hospital lay on the edge of the township of Soweto. It was the only hospital in the area that would admit blacks as well as whites. If she went there, she would immediately have the chance to help some of the thousands of desperately poor people she had seen in Soweto. Yet the other offer—to go to the United States— meant an opportunity to get the kind of education she could never get in her homeland.

Winnie chose to stay in South Africa. It was a fateful decision. One of her co-workers at the hospital was Adelaide Tsukudu, who was engaged to be married to Oliver Tambo. One evening Winnie joined the couple for dinner at a small restaurant. Nelson Mandela walked in, and Oliver called him over. "Nelson, do you recognize this young lady?" he asked teasingly. A photograph of Winnie had again been featured in a magazine when she took the job at Baragwanath Hospital.

Winnie was shy and nervous. Here was this famous man whom she had heard so much about. He was thirty-eight, and she was only twenty, and his charm was legendary. She later said she couldn't remember a thing he said to her.

But Nelson did not forget. Later, he called her at the hospital and asked her to lunch. He took her to an Indian restaurant, where he ordered curry for her. Her eyes watered as she ate it, for she had never tasted anything so hot and spicy. Nelson remarked that he could eat curry all the time. She nodded, forcing the food down. Afterward, she asked her Indian friends how to cook curry.

The next day Nelson phoned again, and soon Winnie was seeing him on a regular basis. But wherever they went, they could never be alone. People constantly came up and sat down with them, wanting to talk with Nelson. Even then, as Winnie later explained, "Life with him was a life without him. He did not even pretend that I would have a special claim to his time." Nelson often sent friends to pick her up at the hospital and bring her to the gym where he was working out. But the relationship deepened.

One day Nelson startled Winnie by saying: "You know, there is a woman, a dressmaker; you must go and see her. She is going to make your wedding gown. How many bridesmaids would you like to have?" It was a strange way to make a marriage proposal, but Winnie understood. There was never any time for "frivolous romance." In response, she merely said, "What time?"

Mandela did speak with her seriously about what marriage would mean. He warned her that life with him would have drawbacks. He was on trial, constantly hounded by the police even while out on bail. If she married him, she would be subject to the same kind of harassment. In addition, he had dedicated his life to obtaining freedom for his people, and this would take precedence over personal feelings. He warned her that it was to be a lifelong commitment, like a call to the ministry. But she probably never dreamed how much suffering and loneliness she would have to endure as the wife of Nelson Mandela.

Because Mandela was under a banning order, he could not travel to Pondoland to speak to Winnie's father. So Winnie returned to tell Columbus herself. His reaction was not entirely favorable. He was honored that Winnie had attracted such a prominent man, but he pointed out that Nelson was a target of the government and on trial for treason. Mandela was also a divorced man with three children.

Columbus was amazed when Winnie told him she had earlier discouraged two other men who had wooed her. In Columbus's eyes they would have made superior husbands. One of them was Mandela's close friend and relative, Kaiser Matanzima. Kaiser was already an important chief in the Transkei. Marrying him would make Winnie part of a royal family.

But Winnie had already made her choice, and she persuaded her father to agree to the marriage. Mandela sent another relative, George Matanzima, to negotiate the bride-price, or *lobola,* with Columbus. The *lobola* is traditionally paid in cattle, and the amount is kept secret from the bride. To this day, Winnie does not know what her *lobola* was.

Mandela, still under a banning order, was granted four days to attend his own wedding in Pondoland in June 1958. Following the Methodist ceremony, the couple celebrated happily with a few relatives and friends. At the end of the four days, Nelson and Winnie headed back to Johannesburg. They moved into a new home in Soweto.

THE ROAD TO SHARPEVILLE

Less than two months later, on August 1, 1958, the main part of the Treason Trial began in Pretoria, the nation's administrative capital. Observers from all over the world came to the courtroom. Day after day, the prosecutors put into evidence every piece of paper they had found on the ANC. The days dragged on; the trial would last for three more years.

Mandela and the other defendants who lived in Soweto had to make the forty-mile trip to Pretoria daily. Each day at the noon recess, Mandela and the other defendants went to a nearby church hall. As the Indian community served lunch for all of them, they discussed new projects. Mandela seized the opportunity to slip away to clandestine meetings at night. Winnie was already finding that being Nelson Mandela's wife took second place to the struggle for a free South Africa.

The government also began to harass the law firm of Mandela and Tambo in an attempt to drive them out of business. They were ordered to close their offices in the Indian section of Johannesburg and move to a township far from the center of town. Mandela remarked that the order "was tantamount to asking us to abandon our practice, to give up the legal service of our people for which we had spent many years training. No attorney worth his salt would agree easily to do so." They ignored the order, and Tambo took over most of the firm's work while Mandela helped out whenever he could.

One happy occasion marked the year 1959. Winnie gave birth to a daughter. According to African custom, the Mandelas asked a chief to give her a proper name. He chose Zenani, which means "What have you brought?" She soon acquired the nickname Zeni.

But 1959 also brought division within the ANC. The Africanists still wanted to keep the organization separate from other nonblack groups. Robert Sobukwe, another of the Treason Trial defendants, was one of those who felt that the blacks had to go it alone. He led a group of ANC members in forming a new organization. This Pan Africanist Congress (PAC) refused cooperation with groups of any other race. Their slogan was "Africa for the Africans."

In 1960, the PAC staged its first major action—a passive resistance campaign against the hated pass laws. Nelson had long been a friend of Sobukwe, but he worried that the PAC was not prepared for what might happen. On March 21, Sobukwe and others walked barefoot to the Orlando police department and burned their passes. They were immediately arrested and jailed.

The PAC's appeals had drawn others to their side. Thirty-five miles from Johannesburg, in Sharpeville, a township outside the city of Vereeniging, a crowd gathered in peaceful protest. When the police arrived, they shot into the crowd, killing 69 people and wounding about 180. Many were shot in the back while trying to flee. Eight women and ten small children were among the casualties. A few days later, police shot more demonstrators in Langa, a township outside Cape Town.

The Sharpeville massacre touched the conscience of the world. The United Nations Security Council passed a resolution blaming the South African government for the shootings. Governments around the world debated possible action against South Africa. Many people proposed sanctions, or economic punishment, such as refusal to trade with the country's businesses. Prices on the Johannesburg Stock Exchange dropped drastically. South Africa's business leaders feared that their country would suffer from the barbaric slaughter at Sharpeville. They were right.

Mandela's fears had come true, but he could not bring himself to blame Sobukwe or the PAC. He felt sick when he heard the news from Sharpeville. Protest demonstrations erupted throughout the country. ANC President Albert Luthuli publicly burned his pass, as did thousands of others. For a few days the government suspended the pass laws, but then reinstated them. All differences between the ANC and the PAC were put aside as Albert Luthuli called for a day of mourning on March 18.

Fearing a new wave of government repression, the ANC leaders decided to send abroad a representative who could operate freely, without the restraint of the South African police. Oliver Tambo was selected for the job, and he fled the country.

On March 30, the South African government showed its

contempt for world opinion. It declared a state of emergency and once again began a series of mass arrests. In the middle of the night, police surrounded the Mandelas' house, shining flashlights into their windows and banging on the front door. It was Winnie's first experience with this kind of brutality, and she was outraged by "these coarse Boer policemen thumbing through our personal belongings, pulling books off shelves, rough handling our possessions and all the time passing derogatory and derisive remarks about kaffirs. It was horrible."

The ANC had been wise to send Tambo abroad, for he was one of the few leaders to escape arrest. On April 8, after declaring that both the ANC and the PAC were a "serious threat to the safety of the public," the government banned both organizations. Just before this happened, the ANC had declared it would carry on its work "until freedom has been won and the scourge of racial discrimination has been banished from our country."

ACQUITTAL

Declaring a state of emergency enabled the government to keep prisoners in jail for as long as it wished. The legal defense team in the Treason Trial resigned in protest. Mandela and another lawyer took over the duties of organizing a proper defense.

It was difficult, for he was now a prisoner in the Pretoria jail, where living conditions were terrible. Each six-by-twelve-foot cell held five prisoners, who had one bucket for drinking water and a second for bodily wastes. Every ten days they were allowed a shower and ten minutes of exercise in the prison yard. Porridge and corn, with a few scraps of meat, were their only food.

Mandela complained to a warden, who responded that prisoners were forbidden to complain during a state of emergency. Mandela quoted from the prison rulebook, and the warden said, "Prison regulations don't require you prisoners to read books!"

Finally, during a session of the Treason Trial, Mandela brought the matter before the chief judge. The prisoners soon began to receive better food and treatment.

Conducting the defense in the Treason Trial marked Mandela's finest hour as a lawyer. For hours, he gave his own testimony and cross-examined government witnesses. All who watched his performance were affected by his dignity, his command of the facts, and his regard for the law. He frequently gave long, thoughtful answers in response to questioning by the judge and prosecuting attorneys.

In one exchange, the prosecutor tried to show that Mandela knew that the actions of the ANC would bring about violence by the government. Mandela replied: "Yes, the Congress was of that view, my lords. We did expect force to be used . . . but as far as we are concerned we took the precautions to ensure that the violence will not come from our side."

The judge also asked: "Well, as a matter of fact, isn't your freedom a direct threat to the Europeans?"

Mandela answered: "No, it is not a direct threat to the Europeans. We are not anti-white; we are against white supremacy and in struggling against white supremacy we have the support of some sections of the European population. . . . We said that the campaign we were about to launch was not directed against any racial group. It was . . . directed against laws which we considered unjust."

In August the state of emergency was lifted, and the prisoners were released. Each day after the trial, Nelson went home. But life in the Mandela household was, as usual, hardly normal. Winnie recalled, "There has never been a stage in my life where it was my husband and I and the children. He would come home from court and say, 'Darling, I brought my friends here to taste your lovely cooking,' and he would pitch up with ten people and we would have one chop in the fridge."

In December 1960, Mandela heard that his younger son, Makgatho, had fallen ill in the Transkei. Though his banning order prevented him from traveling, he disguised himself and hurried to be at his son's bedside. It was an unfortunate time, for while he was gone, Winnie gave birth to a second daughter, Zindziswa, nicknamed Zindzi. But Mandela soon returned.

In March of the following year, the trial finally ended. Winnie sat nervously in the gallery of the courtroom waiting for the verdict to be announced. It was possible that Nelson could be found guilty and given the death penalty. A lesser penalty was life imprisonment. Winnie could hardly believe her ears as she heard the judge say the state had failed to prove the defendants had followed a policy of violence. Although the ANC showed a "strong left-wing tendency," continued the judge, the state had not proved it was Communist or that the Freedom Charter advocated a Communist state. There was no treason involved. He looked at the assembled defendants: "You are found Not Guilty. You may go."

The friends and relatives of the defendants cheered wildly. They began to shout, "Nkosi Sikeleli Afrika," which means "God Bless Africa."

5 THE BLACK PIMPERNEL

Despite the constant provocations, the African National Congress had clung to the ideal of nonviolence. But events within South Africa at the end of the 1950s and the beginning of the 1960s would change this strategy.

The Sharpeville massacre showed that the South African government had taken an increasingly brutal line toward demonstrators. Now even greater violence erupted over the government's homelands policy.

The government had adopted its plan to set up Bantustans, or independent homelands, in the former reserves. Over the years, the country's black population had increased. South Africa's industries could not use all of the black workers. The government planned to rid the country of this "surplus" by relocating people in the Bantustans and then declaring them independent. In these out-of-the-way areas, black Africans would no longer cause trouble for South Africa's white government.

The Transkei was one of these Bantustans. Kaiser Matanzima, Mandela's friend and kinsman, accepted the government's offer to be the leader of the Transkei. His brother George was his chief adviser.

To the members of the ANC, any blacks who cooperated

in the Bantustan relocation efforts were traitors. Mandela was particularly saddened that two of his closest friends were among them.

The situation erupted into violence when blacks in the Transkei began to attack the government-chosen chiefs. Kaiser Matanzima called in police to protect his authority, and they burned the huts of many of the people who opposed him. Hundreds of people were arrested. A delegation came to Mandela's home in Soweto to seek his help, but he could do nothing. Matanzima had turned his back on everything that Mandela prized—dignity, freedom, rights for all Africans.

Similarly, Winnie's father, Columbus Madikizela, accepted a government post in the Pondoland region of the Transkei. He too was threatened by protesters who rose in revolt. The government sent in troops, who brutally quelled the fighting. Winnie did not speak to her father again for years.

The Mandelas were not the only family split apart by the Bantustan policy. Many blacks continued to resist government-sponsored black leaders like Kaiser Matanzima. Others found that cooperation brought them power and prosperity, for the government rewarded its supporters. Combined with the division between the ANC and the PAC, the homelands struggle began the tragic cycle of violence in which blacks fought and killed other blacks. It continues to be a major problem in today's South Africa.

GOING UNDERGROUND

Two weeks before the end of the Treason Trial, the government allowed Mandela's banning order to expire. Possibly it was an oversight on the part of a government official who expected Mandela to be convicted in the trial. In any case, he was now free, for the first time in years, to go wherever he wanted within the country. Perhaps more important, he could appear in public at political gatherings.

He asked Winnie to pack a suitcase for him. She went inside the house, but by the time she returned with the suitcase, he had already left. Later, a friend came to pick up the suitcase. The next day, March 25, 1961, she read in the afternoon newspapers that he had gone to attend the All-in-African Conference.

The conference had been called because the government was about to declare South Africa a republic. It would leave the British Commonwealth of Nations, a group of British colonies and former colonies, and thus be free of any restraints on its actions. The All-in-African Conference assembled 1,400 delegates, political and cultural leaders of black South Africa, to discuss what to do about this new development.

The appearance of Nelson Mandela electrified the crowd. This was the first time in nine years that he had appeared before a public meeting. The conference demanded that a new constitution be drafted, setting up a government with no color bar. The delegates decided that if their demands were not met, they would call for a three-day "stay-at-home" to begin on the same day the republic was established, May 31, 1961. Mandela was chosen to organize the stay-at-home.

He returned to Pretoria to hear the not guilty verdict at the trial. Then he made the decision to go underground, to operate outside the law, for he knew that the government would soon ban him again.

"That was the last I saw of my husband as a family man," Winnie later wrote. He had no time to discuss his decision with her. But she suspected it when she found that he had paid six months' rent on the house in advance and that he had taken their car to be repaired. He left it parked outside the house and simply disappeared. Telling her where he was going would only endanger her.

Throughout April and May 1961, Mandela toured the country secretly with Walter Sisulu. He found a welcome in many homes, even though the penalty for harboring a fugitive was harsh. At night he visited groups who had assembled in secret to hear his call to action.

He also sent letters to the head of the government, Hendrik Verwoerd, and to the leader of the main opposition party in the country's parliament. Mandela told Verwoerd, "We have no illusions about the counter-measures your government might take. . . . We are not deterred by threats of force and violence."

To the opposition leader, Mandela pleaded for support in the call for a constitutional convention. "It is still not too late," he wrote. "A call [from you] for a National Convention . . . could well be the turning point in our country's history. It would isolate the Nationalist government and reveal for all time that it is a minority government." Neither letter drew a reply. The preparations for the stay-at-home continued.

The government took strong measures to disrupt the plans. Its security police had developed a highly effective spy network, and they arrested some ten thousand people. Meetings were banned and printing presses seized. Mandela continued to elude capture, passing through police roadblocks even though his tall, striking figure made him easily recognizable. He went from township to township, speaking and distributing leaflets.

As the day for the stay-at-home drew closer, foreign journalists went to South Africa, expecting another Sharpeville. The government also prepared for violence, sending troops to guard white areas of the cities. The London *Observer* described the climate of fear that had come over the country: "Heavy army vehicles carrying equipment and supplies moved in a steady stream . . . helicopters hovered over African residential areas and trained searchlights on houses [and] yards. . . . Police vans . . . broadcast statements that Africans who went on strike would be [fired] and forced out of the town."

Mandela insisted that all protests were to be strictly nonviolent. On the first day of the demonstration, hundreds of thousands risked arrest and the loss of their jobs by participating. Even so, the stay-at-home was a disappointment. The government had done its job well. Mandela acknowledged this by calling off the strike on the second day.

"THE STRUGGLE IS MY LIFE"

The big story for newspapers now became Mandela's attempt to elude the government. For the next year and a half he continued his work underground, appearing for brief meetings and then disappearing again. He used false names and many disguises. At one point he drove a car in a chauffeur's uniform and cap, knowing that police would not give him a second glance.

He had many narrow escapes. Once, he had to slide down a rope from a second-story window while police were entering the building by the front door. In the black townships, stories about him circulated. People were gleeful that for once, a black man could defy the government. Newspapers began to call him "the Black Pimpernel," after a fictional character, the Scarlet Pimpernel, who always escaped from his enemies.

Mandela wrote a letter to a journalist, explaining that going underground was the only way he could continue the struggle for his people's rights. "I have had to . . . live as an outlaw in my own land. I have had to abandon my profession and live in poverty, as many of my people are doing. . . . The struggle is my life. I will continue fighting for freedom until the end of my days."

One of his favorite hiding places was a farm outside Johannesburg, called Lilliesleaf. It was owned by a white man who opposed apartheid and allowed the banned ANC to use it for meetings. Winnie brought their two daughters there to be with their father on a few treasured occasions. He would take them on walks through the fruit orchards and row them down the little stream on the farm.

Whenever he was near Johannesburg, he tried to see his family. Winnie never knew when she would be awakened by a soft knock at her bedroom window in the early hours of the morning. If it was too dangerous to go home, he tried to have her brought to him. She would receive a message telling her to meet a car at a certain place. The driver would take her somewhere else, where she would switch cars—sometimes taking as many as ten cars before coming to a house where he was

61

hiding. But they never had more than a brief time together before he was on the run again.

On one occasion, someone came to Winnie at work and told her to drive to a particular corner. When she got there, a tall man in a chauffeur's white coat and peaked cap opened the door and got in. Even she hadn't recognized him until he took off the cap and smiled.

Such moments were painfully brief. They had been married for less than three years when he went underground, and all that time he had been on trial for treason. "I had so little time to love him," Winnie later wrote, "and that love has survived all these years of separation."

THE SPEAR OF THE NATION

The successful government crackdown on the stay-at-home was a watershed for the ANC. It was clear that the government would not be moved by any nonviolent protests. Later that same year, in October 1961, Albert Luthuli was awarded the Nobel Peace Prize in recognition of his nonviolent efforts to obtain full rights for South Africa's blacks. South Africa's government condemned the award, though it reluctantly allowed Luthuli and his wife to go to Oslo, Norway, to accept it.

The award was a hollow victory for the ANC, an organization that could not operate publicly anywhere in South Africa. Many blacks, especially the young, wanted to go beyond nonviolence and take stronger action—acts of terrorism against whites. Some of the ANC's leaders felt that their policy of peaceful protest was losing the support of the youth.

Mandela was reluctant to turn to violence. He knew how important nonviolence had been in bringing international sympathy for the anti-apartheid struggle. But now that the government had outlawed all legal methods of protest, there seemed to be no other way for the freedom movement to turn.

With the blessing of the ANC leaders, Mandela organized a new group that would work apart from the ANC. The group would become known as Umkhonto we Sizwe, "the Spear of the Nation." Umkhonto's mission was to carry out sabotage within South Africa. Its targets would be government installations and buildings, but it would try to ensure that no lives would be lost.

Umkhonto carried out its first action in December 1961, on the anniversary of the Boer victory at Blood River. Bombs went off in power plants and government offices in Johannesburg and Port Elizabeth. One of the saboteurs was killed in the explosions.

At the time of the first action, Umkhonto issued a manifesto that stated, "We . . . have always sought . . . to achieve liberation without bloodshed and civil clash. . . . The time comes in the life of any nation when there remain only two choices: submit or fight. That time has now come to South Africa."

SEEKING ALLIES ABROAD

Umkhonto's first action thrilled many black Africans, but the government intensified its search for Nelson Mandela. Early in January 1962, he slipped out of the country and met Oliver Tambo in Nigeria. Merely leaving South Africa without permission was illegal, and the government added this to the list of Nelson's "crimes."

Tambo had arranged for Mandela to speak at the Pan African Freedom Conference of black African nations in Addis Ababa, Ethiopia. Mandela told of the many actions that the ANC had taken to change the government's policies and then described the brutal repression that had resulted. He appealed to the delegates to continue their nations' support. Some had already boycotted South African goods and had given asylum to black Africans, such as Tambo, who had fled the country.

After the conference, Mandela and Tambo toured many countries in Africa. At all stops they met with enthusiasm for their cause. Mandela was inspired by the success of nationalist movements in winning independence in the other African nations. In Algeria, he arranged for military training for

Umkhonto recruits. After the African tour he went on to London, where he was received by leaders of the British Labor party.

Mandela had never been outside South Africa before, and the experience was a revelation to him. For the first time he was truly a free man: "Wherever I went I was treated like a human being. In the African states I saw black and white mingling peacefully and happily in hotels, cinemas: trading in the same areas, using the same public transport, and living in the same residential areas." He dreamed that one day he would see all of those things in South Africa.

Personally, he must have yearned to remain outside his own country—not only free but idolized as the leader of the freedom struggle in South Africa. But he knew that he was a symbol of hope to his people. He returned to South Africa as secretly as he had left.

CAPTURED

For a time Mandela rested at Lilliesleaf Farm, this time joined by his younger son Makgatho, who was twelve. Mandela tried to make up in a few days for the years that he had lost with his son. He and Makgatho swam, walked, and talked together, and Mandela taught his son how to shoot a rifle. When the time came for Makgatho to leave, his father told him that he would go to school in another African country. Education was all-important, and no black youth could now get a proper one in South Africa. In Mandela's lifetime, things had gotten worse, not better.

Umkhonto's sabotage campaign had continued during his absence. He met with its other members to plan new actions. Then he traveled to Natal Province to visit Albert Luthuli. Luthuli was disturbed by the Umkhonto policy and upset that he had not been consulted about its activities. Nelson told him that the decision to exclude him and other leaders was made to protect the ANC. If any of Umkhonto's members were cap-

In the Transkei, Mandela's birthplace, Xhosa women pass a cluster of straw-thatched huts, similar to those in which he had lived as a child.

Left: As a young man, Mandela took up boxing for exercise.

Below: To protest the laws of apartheid, Mandela and other demonstrators burned the passbooks South African law required all blacks to carry.

TREASON TRIAL

DECEMBER 1956

The ACCUSED

Above: A photo-montage shows the defendants charged with high treason by the South African government in 1956. Mandela is standing tall in the center of the third row.

Right: Nelson and Winnie were married in Pondoland, in 1958.

Above: In August 1960, Nelson and Winnie rejoice at the news that the state of emergency has been lifted and the treason trial prisoners may be released.

Right: Finally acquitted in 1961, after the three-year treason trial, Mandela began moving through the country, organizing a "stay-at-home."

Above: Winnie Mandela leads Mandela's mother past guards outside the Pretoria courthouse where he was sentenced to life imprisonment in June 1964.

Right: In the prison yard at Robben Island, Mandela is seen making prison clothes.

Thousands of people—
including many schoolchildren—
took part in the angry
demonstrations in
Soweto in the
summer of 1976.

Steve Biko, a Black Consciousness leader, died in September 1977, while in police custody after the Soweto protests.

Below, left: In Soweto, on February 10, 1985, Zindzi Mandela is carried jubilantly to the stage to deliver her father's proud rejection of the government's offer of freedom.

Right: A 1989 photograph shows Winnie Mandela with the Mandela Football Club. The club was disbanded, but members continued to serve as her bodyguards.

After twenty-seven years in prison, Mandela and his supporters can celebrate,"Free at Last!"

Nelson and Winnie Mandela
respond to cheering crowds at the
time of his release from prison
on February 11, 1990.

A photograph from the late 1980s shows Mandela's first wife, Eveline (seated, left), and son, Makgatho (standing), with other family members at their home.

African National Congress leaders Oliver Tambo (left) and Walter Sisulu (below)

Right: In May 1990, Mandela and South African State President F. W. de Clerk appeared together in public before beginning talks between the ANC and the government.

Crowds of supporters, left, greeted Mandela at rallies throughout his 1990 American tour.

President George Bush, below, greets Mandela at the White House in June 1990.

*Mangosuthu Gatsha Buthelezi is the founder
and leader of the Inkatha Freedom party,
a Zulu rights organization.*

Violence has continued in South Africa,
often between supporters of the rival ANC
and Inkatha, and as seen here, the police
have not always been able to stop it.

tured, the ANC leaders could prove they knew nothing about the organization's work.

The experience of real freedom may have changed Nelson. He let down his guard, perhaps thinking that the government believed he would never return. He met with a group of friends for a party. Afterward, one of them drove him toward Johannesburg. The police were waiting. American newspapers later published reports that agents working for the United States Central Intelligence Agency (CIA) had tipped off the police about where to find Mandela.

The driver of Mandela's car saw the police coming up from behind. Mandela's mind raced. He considered jumping out of the car and trying to run. But another look showed two more police cars. Three all together in this lonely spot showed that they knew who they were chasing. The government would be pleased to announce that he was killed trying to escape.

So he tried to bluff it through. When the police pulled his car over, he gave a false name. The police sergeant shook his head and called him Nelson Mandela. The game was up. After seventeen months as a fugitive, the Black Pimpernel was captured on August 5, 1962. He was imprisoned in the Johannesburg Fort.

On August 8, Mandela stood in court listening without emotion as the charges were read. He was accused of inciting workers to strike in 1961 and of leaving the country illegally. He must have been relieved; the charges did not mention his activities with Umkhonto. Winnie watched from the public gallery as he was led away in handcuffs.

The slogan "Free Mandela" appeared on the walls of township houses throughout South Africa. Beyond the nation's borders, people who admired him called for his release. International organizations condemned South Africa once more.

To no avail. Protests did not move South Africa's government, which only cracked down harder. It banned hundreds of people who had any connection with Mandela. This time the banning orders were more severe than ever before. It was made a crime for one banned person to speak to another. Husbands and wives who were banned had to apply for permission from the government to speak. All gatherings that supported Mandela were banned.

On October 22, 1962, Mandela's trial opened in Pretoria. A crowd had assembled in the street outside the courthouse. As he emerged from the police van, he raised his fist and called, "Amandla!" (Power!), to which the answer came "Ngawethu!" (To the People!).

Mandela began by telling the judge he would carry on his own defense. He challenged the authority of the court to try him. "I consider myself neither legally nor morally bound to obey laws made by a parliament in which I have no representation. In a political trial such as this one, which involves a clash of the aspirations of the African people and those of whites, the country's courts . . . cannot be impartial and fair."

As the trial went on, Mandela cross-examined government witnesses. He asked why his letter to the prime minister had not been answered. He suggested it was "scandalous" that the prime minister of a country would refuse to answer a letter written on behalf of the majority of the population.

He defended his role in calling for a convention to write a color-free constitution on the grounds that he was acting to prevent violence in the country. "The government has set out not to treat with us, not to heed us, not to talk to us, but rather to present us as wild, dangerous revolutionaries, intent on disorder and riot, incapable of being dealt with in any way save by mustering an overwhelming force against us."

Mandela was found guilty on both counts—inciting workers to strike and leaving the country illegally—on October 25, 1962. At his sentencing he told the court: "It has not been easy for me . . . to separate myself from my wife and children . . . to take up the life of a man hunted continually by the police . . . but there comes a time, as it came in my life, when a man . . . can only live the life of an outlaw because the government has so decreed to use the law to impose a state of outlawry upon him. I

66

was driven to this situation and I do not regret having taken the decisions I did take." Afterward he was sentenced to five years in prison. But before he completed his term, the government would charge that he was behind the Umkhonto operation.

6 A LIFE SENTENCE

Mandela began to serve his five-year prison sentence at Pretoria Central Prison. It was a gloomy place, but life there was not particularly harsh. He had three meals of mashed mealie corn every day, and was assigned to sew mailbags. As he had told Winnie, "suffering in jail is nothing compared to suffering outside jail"—the suffering that all nonwhite South Africans endured every day.

But a few months after his arrival, Mandela and three other men were abruptly taken away in a police van. The three others had also committed acts that the government regarded as threats to public safety. All were black. One was a union organizer, another was a newspaper reporter, and the third was a troublesome older man who had complained about the jailers' conduct.

They didn't know where they were going until they were shifted from the van to a boat—that could mean only that their destination was the most feared prison in South Africa, Robben Island.

Robben Island's jailers made every effort to break the spirit of their prisoners. When Mandela and the others arrived, several guards armed with rifles took charge of them. They lined up the prisoners and began to shout, "Huck, huck, huck!" to hurry them forward, as if they were cattle being herded through a field.

But Mandela knew that if he were to survive in prison, he must always preserve the sense that he was a man, entitled to the rights that even prisoners had. He and the older prisoner refused to run.

The guards prodded them with their rifles, shouting threats. Mandela had steeled himself against such treatment. He did not turn, or strike out, or run. They could not make him run.

Inside the prison, they were ordered to strip off their clothes. They obeyed but stood calmly as a chief guard appeared and began to shout at them. He called them "boys." Naked, Mandela was no less dignified. He told the guard that he would report him to higher authorities. The man was thunderstruck. No prisoner had ever dared to treat him this way. But he did not strike Mandela, for both knew that prison regulations forbade such treatment.

After that, the guards at Robben Island knew that Mandela would be a hard man to break. He had won the first confrontation, and in doing so had ensured that they would be careful with him.

A SPECTACULAR RAID

Though Mandela had been jailed, Umkhonto continued its sabotage campaign. The government retaliated with more and more arrests, more and more harsh laws and punishments. The punishment merely for membership in an "unlawful organization" was changed from five years to the death penalty. That included everyone in the ANC.

So-called political prisoners didn't have to do anything at all for the government to keep them in jail. A new law made it possible to "detain" such prisoners after they had completed their legal jail sentences. After Robert Sobukwe, the leader of the PAC, finished serving a three-year jail term, he was immediately sent to an isolated hut on Robben Island.

The security police were rounding up suspects right and left. Walter Sisulu was arrested six times during 1962. Finally, he too went underground, as Mandela had done earlier.

The government made its most spectacular raid on July 11, 1963. The police had finally discovered Lilliesleaf Farm, the peaceful estate at Rivonia that served as the headquarters of the outlawed ANC. Late that night, concealed in a bakery truck and a dry cleaner's van, armed police and attack dogs crept onto the grounds. They burst through the front door of the house, interrupting a meeting. Walter Sisulu leaped out of a window but faced a ring of policemen and attack dogs. More than a dozen others, including several whites who sympathized with the ANC's cause, were also arrested.

But more important, the police found at Rivonia a file of documents that revealed many of the details of the planning that had gone into Umkhonto's sabotage campaign. Finally, the government had proof that Mandela had taken part in treason. And the penalty was death.

ACCUSED NUMBER ONE

The "Rivonia trial" that resulted from this discovery began under the tightest security. The government would not even give the names of the accused to lawyers who volunteered to defend them. The day before the trial, the prosecutor allowed the defense team to visit Pretoria prison. Only then did they discover who their clients were.

Mandela, secretly transferred from Robben Island, was among them. The lawyers and those who were captured at Lilliesleaf were shocked at the sight of him. He had lost forty pounds, and the prison uniform of boy's shorts and shirt hung limply on his body. His skin had a yellowish tinge. But he still retained his impressive bearing. Being with Sisulu and his other political allies seemed to have a tonic effect on him. As the days went on, he gained weight and became his old self again.

Mandela was serene and confident, though he faced a death penalty. His manner affected even the hard-bitten Afrikaner jailers. When a guard treated him roughly and Mandela protested, the guard replied, "When you are the government, you will do it to us." It was the remark of someone who believed Mandela and his cohorts would eventually win their struggle.

The defendants were charged with recruiting people for sabotage and the violent overthrow of the government. One by one, they were called before the court. Significantly, Nelson was "Accused Number One." He stood and in a firm voice declared, "The government should be in the dock, not me. I plead not guilty." As did the rest.

For five long months, the prosecution carefully presented its case. Its evidence included maps found at Rivonia marked with the locations of police stations, electric power plants, railroad lines, and other possible targets. Among the documents was a diary Nelson had kept during his tour of African countries. It contained his plans to train guerrilla fighters in Algeria.

Mandela and the others knew that the proof against them was solid. Ignoring their own fate, they decided to turn the trial into a forum for airing all their grievances against South Africa's racist government. They could not be stopped from speaking now, and reporters and diplomats from many foreign countries were present in the courtroom to hear and report their words.

This freedom—to speak without fear—was one they had rarely enjoyed. It was elating. Dancing on the edge of a death sentence, the defendants even joked. An Afrikaner guard named Swanepoel stood at the door of the room where the defendants were allowed to speak with their attorneys. To keep Swanepoel from hearing, they sometimes exchanged notes, immediately burning them in an ashtray.

With a great show of secrecy, Mandela handed a note to a comrade. After reading it, he crumpled the paper and put it in the ashtray. Swanepoel could not resist. He rushed forward, mumbling something about preventing fires in the courthouse, and seized the note. When he unfolded it, his face reddened. Mandela had written, "Isn't Swanepoel a fine-looking chap?"

AN ELOQUENT DEFENSE

As the prosecution finished its case, the trial recessed for a month to allow the defense to prepare. Lawyers and prisoners argued over whether or not to allow Mandela and the others to testify. If they did, the prosecution could cross-examine them, and the prosecutor was a skilled, sarcastic questioner who would try to trip them up.

Mandela insisted that he and the others be allowed to speak. As a lawyer himself, he said he realized that his attorneys' first concern was to present an effective case for saving their clients' lives. But he had a higher purpose: his political beliefs. He had fought for freedom, and would go down continuing that fight. No matter what the risk, he and the others would tell the truth for the world to hear.

Thus, Mandela led off the case for the defense. He described how he had organized Umkhonto and gave his reasons. He flatly declared: "I do not . . . deny that I planned sabotage. I did not plan it in a spirit of recklessness, nor because I have any love of violence. I planned it as a result of a calm and sober assessment of the political situation that had arisen after many years of tyranny, exploitation, and oppression of my people by the Whites." However, Mandela specifically denied the involvement of Umkhonto in many of the 193 acts of sabotage cited in the prosecution case.

He went on to describe the history of the ANC's efforts to change the apartheid laws, even after the ANC was declared an illegal organization: "The African people were not part of the government and did not make the laws by which they were governed. We believed in the words of the Universal Declaration of Human Rights, that 'the will of the people shall be the basis of authority of the Government,' and for us to accept the banning was equivalent to accepting the silencing of the Africans for all time."

Mandela pointed out the violent government response, at Sharpeville and other places, to the ANC's attempts to use nonviolent means to change the system. According to Mandela, Umkhonto was established because "I and some colleagues came to the conclusion that as violence in this country was inevitable, it would be unrealistic and wrong for African leaders to continue preaching peace and non-violence at a time when the Government met our peaceful demands with force."

He took up the government accusation that the ANC was Communist because it had accepted Communist aid and that the ANC's aims were the same as those of the Communist party: "The ANC, unlike the Communist Party, admitted Africans only as members. Its chief goal was, and is, for the African people to win unity and full political rights. The Communist Party's main aim, on the other hand, was to remove the capitalists and to replace them with a working-class government. The Communist Party sought to emphasize class distinctions whilst the ANC seeks to harmonize them. This is a vital distinction."

After four hours of speaking, Mandela left his notes and ended his defense with the statement: "During my lifetime I have dedicated myself to the struggle of the African people. I have fought against white domination, and I have fought against black domination. I have cherished the ideal of a democratic and free society in which all people live together in harmony and with equal opportunities. It is an ideal which I hope to live for and to achieve. But if it needs be, it is an ideal for which I am prepared to die."

LIFE IMPRISONMENT

The trial recessed again to let the judge decide the case. Amazingly, while Mandela waited, he was able to concentrate his mind on a totally different matter. He was taking tests sent to him by the law school of London University. He was attempting to earn an advanced law degree. (Even more amazingly, he passed the tests.)

On June 11, 1964, the court reassembled. The judge had

73

reached a verdict. Winnie arrived with her daughters and Nelson's aged mother. Zeni and Zindzi, aged five and four, were not permitted inside.

The judge intoned the verdicts slowly. Mandela and all but one of the other defendants were found guilty on all four counts. The judge would announce their sentences the next day. Mandela waved to Winnie and his mother as he was led away.

Mandela was fully prepared for the death sentence. He told his lawyer that he would declare that his death would inspire his people in continuing the struggle. He would not allow his lawyers to appeal the sentence.

The news of the guilty verdict spread like fire on the South African veld. In the townships, leaflets urged people to protest. Slogans were painted on walls overnight. Around the world, newspapers condemned South Africa's government. The United Nations had already voted to urge that all the prisoners be freed. Only one vote—South Africa's—had opposed the resolution.

At dawn a crowd of people gathered around the courthouse. Police set up roadblocks to prevent more from coming into the city. Their banners proclaimed, "We Are Proud of Our Leaders" and "No Tears: Our Future Is Bright."

Inside, the courtroom was silent except for the judge's voice. He detailed the charges again and then said he had decided to show leniency. A whoosh of air escaped from the spectators' lips. Leniency! He would not condemn them to death! The sentence was life imprisonment.

Mandela turned, smiled at Winnie and his mother, and gave the thumbs-up ANC salute that meant *Afrika!* Winnie took her cue from him. When she came out on the courthouse steps, she gave the crowd a dazzling smile. A reporter thought she looked like an African queen, and the people who saw her cheered in sympathy.

The crowd shouted again, "Amandla! Ngawethu!" as the prisoners were driven away. Carrying her daughters, Winnie tried to push through to let them catch a last glimpse of their father. But suddenly she felt a hand on her shoulder. It was a security policeman. In the midst of the confusion and cheering, he reminded her that her permit to attend the trial expired at twelve o'clock.

"Here I was," she later recalled, "and there is this man with his hand on my shoulder repeating that I must go back to Johannesburg! All I could do was kick him and ignore him. Can you imagine! The last day! My husband is sentenced to life and I must think in terms of permits and the time of day."

Nelson Mandela was forty-five years old. He faced spending the rest of his life in prison. But prison would not dim his spirit, nor his importance to South Africa's future. The world would not forget him.

7 PRISONER NUMBER 446/64

Mandela was returned to Robben Island. It was a bleak, wind-swept fort in the Atlantic Ocean off Cape Town. Long ago, tunnels had been dug under the rocky surface to allow defend-ers to move from place to place unseen, and the island was ringed with a battery of cannons facing outward.

At first, Mandela and the other political prisoners were kept in the old part of the jail, which had stood since the early days of colonization. A thirty-foot-high wall separated the po-litical prisoners from the ordinary criminals. Guards with Ger-man shepherd dogs patrolled the corridors of the prison buildings.

Each prisoner had an identity card. Mandela's identified him as prisoner number 446/64, and gave his offense as sabo-tage. His cell was about seven feet square. The only light came from a weak bulb in the ceiling. He had no bed, only a bedroll and two blankets. A pail for body wastes stood in a corner, but he had to wait for meals to get anything to drink.

THE PRISON ROUTINE
The day began before sunrise, when the prisoners were given breakfast. Even here, distinctions between races were enforced.

76

At breakfast, each racial group was served porridge made from a different kind of grain. The Indians and coloreds got a spoonful of sugar and some bread. The blacks received only a half-spoonful and no bread. The rest of their meals consisted of corn, soup, and black coffee. Occasionally, vegetables and a small piece of meat were added.

The black prisoners spent virtually all their time in the solitary cells, and they were warned by the guards to be silent—no singing or praying aloud. They had nothing to do but sit in silence. When the prisoners were permitted to bathe, they were forced to run naked to the washroom in the new part of the prison. In the cells, they wore only uniform shirts and shorts that provided little protection against the winter cold.

Mandela knew how to keep his spirit alive—he began to petition for better conditions. The prisoners demanded the right to leave their cells for exercise, to be allowed to speak to one another, to have fresh water in the cells, and to be given better food. They won a small victory when they were allowed to crush rocks as exercise, but the penalty for speaking was the loss of three meals. Sometimes, however, they could briefly trade messages under the noise of the hammering.

In the summer, they were taken outside to a limestone quarry. Their chains were removed, and they cut limestone and loaded the blocks onto a truck. The lime pit was like an oven, and the stone reflected the sun's glare, so the men were scorched from above and below. After a long day in the pits, the men were white from limestone dust and completely exhausted.

Yet even in such conditions, the prisoners developed a sense of comradeship. In brief snatches of conversation, they traded whatever news they had heard. As they ate, they discussed their political beliefs. Some were from organizations other than the ANC, and they talked about their different approaches to changing the cruel society of South Africa. In ordinary prisons, inmates learn new criminal methods from each other; at Robben Island, they developed new ways to win the struggle for freedom.

Robben inmates who were transferred to other prisons were constantly asked, "Do you know Nelson Mandela? What kind of man is he?" One prisoner, interviewed about his experiences, said, "Nelson is a very friendly and warm person to meet, but one also feels that he maintains a distance. To get to know him really well takes time."

The prisoner added that Mandela found out if anyone else was having problems with the prison regimen. He would take care to spend time with such people, encouraging them. For in prison, Nelson had himself attained the self-discipline he hoped for. He learned to control his anger completely, so the guards could never provoke him.

Sometimes he took out his anger on the limestone rock in the quarry. He told a biographer, "You begin the task briskly, full of zest, song and swing, but soon the hard rock takes it all away. . . . Then the singing changes to swearing."

Once, when Mandela became sick and too weak to lift the rocks, he was ordered to spend six days in solitary confinement on a diet of water in which rice had been boiled. Through sheer force of will, he fought to keep up his physical and mental strength. He set for himself a routine of physical exercise.

But the work in the dusty quarry had damaged Mandela's eyesight, and he began to develop more serious health problems: high blood pressure and back trouble. Even more difficult for him was the concern he felt for Winnie and his children. By prison regulations, no one under sixteen could visit him; he would not see either of his daughters for more than ten years.

WINNIE ALONE

Winnie was devastated by Mandela's imprisonment. Worse than anything else, she remembered, was the loneliness, which was "worse than fear—the most wretchedly painful illness that the body and mind could be subjected to."

Nelson was permitted to write her one letter of five hundred words every six months. The first one she received raised her spirits. She read it over and over until the second letter came six months later.

Finally, she was allowed to visit him. She and Albertina Sisulu traveled the thousand miles from Johannesburg to Cape Town. Guards warned her that she would not be permitted to speak in Xhosa or in any other language the guards did not understand. She was allowed to talk only about family matters.

Nelson appeared at the other side of a small, dim window; they spoke by telephone. She told him of Zeni, who was six and enrolled in school. Zindzi, four-and-a-half, went to kindergarten but was unhappy there. Nelson was eager for any news, urging her to describe everything she could remember about their lives. Both tried to be cheerful, but now that they saw each other in person they were reminded again that they would never be able to spend a normal life together.

Nelson warned her that the government would make her a special target of harassment. She would have to remain strong and control her feelings at all times. Any misconduct on her part would be magnified. At the end of a half hour, the guard called out "Time's up!" So short, so poor a substitute for a real life together!

Winnie tried to throw herself into her work at the Child Welfare Society. But in 1965, the government imposed a five-year ban on her. She was restricted to the township of Orlando, within Soweto, and thus had to give up her job with the society. When she found other work, the government pressured employers to fire her. One store manager told her he had been informed by the police that she could work there only if she divorced Nelson.

For both Nelson and Winnie, one of the most terrible things to endure was the hardships their children had to face. Under the terms of her ban, Winnie was forbidden to enter any educational institution and so had to ask relatives to take the children to school. Whoever showed up with one of Nelson Mandela's children was taken to the headquarters of the security police and interrogated. In addition, the government pressured the schools to expel the children soon after they were accepted.

Finally, Winnie sent Zeni and Zindzi to school in Swaziland, a small black nation adjoining South Africa. It was hard to send her children away, but it was the only way they could receive the education that their parents wanted for them. When her daughters came home on holidays, she gave them all the love she could.

In 1966, Winnie visited Nelson for the second time. The government refused to let them meet unless she obtained an official pass—something she had defiantly refused to do ever since Nelson burned his. But meeting him was more important than a piece of paper. She got the pass.

It had been almost two years since their last meeting. Yet their love remained as strong as ever. They looked at each other, separated by the glass pane, and their eyes told what both knew—the desire to be alone, to touch, to kiss. Yet they had not even the privacy to speak without guards hovering near, listening to every word.

The government continued to harass Winnie, imprisoning her for four days after the second visit because she refused to give her name and address to a policeman. Another time, she spent six months in jail, having been convicted of speaking with another banned person who had brought her daughters to see her.

Wherever she went, police followed, looking for any infractions of the countless rules of apartheid and banning. One day, she was undressing in her bedroom when a policeman barged in. As he put his hand on her shoulder, she turned and shoved him. "I don't know how he landed on his neck," she said. "I remember seeing his legs up in the air and him screaming, and the whole dressing stand falling on him."

Six policemen waiting outside responded to their comrade's cries for help. Winnie was charged with assault. But when the judge saw her standing next to the burly Afrikaner policeman, the case was dismissed.

Hearing of the incident, Nelson appreciated his wife's

spunk and spirit. The story spread among the other political prisoners on Robben Island. Even though they were forbidden to read newspapers and magazines, news from the outside world continued to seep through.

SORROWS FOR NELSON

Sometimes, the prisoners overheard the guards' conversations about current news. They also noticed that the guards' behavior toward them varied according to what was happening outside. The guards were unusually harsh when they felt threatened—as in 1966, when black revolution broke out in Namibia, a neighboring territory controlled by South Africa. Later that year, South Africa's prime minister was assassinated by a white man. The guards feared it was part of a plot and treated the prisoners cruelly.

In 1967, Nelson received the sad news of the death of his old friend Albert Luthuli. South Africa's first Nobel Peace Prize recipient had been banned by his government and confined to a small town in his native region. Each day he took a walk along a railway track, and one day he was found dead, apparently struck by a train. Mandela was not the only one to suspect that Luthuli had not absent-mindedly stood in the path of an oncoming train.

The next year, Nelson's mother died at home in the Transkei. She had been in ill health for years, and again he grieved that the political cause he chose had kept him from easing her last days by being with her. He applied for permission to attend her funeral, but in another of its heedlessly cruel acts, the government refused.

Three months later, Winnie described the funeral and burial of his mother when she visited Nelson. They could not have imagined that they would not see one another for nearly two years. For the government now decided to punish him further by jailing Winnie.

On May 12, 1969, Winnie was awakened by the police at 2:00 A.M. Policemen searched the house, even removing Zeni and Zindzi, who were home on holiday, from their beds so that they could look under the sheets. They confiscated all of Nelson's old clothes, his typewriter, and every book in the house. When they finished, they told Winnie that she was being detained. Winnie was refused permission to contact anyone—lawyer, minister, relatives, or friends. No one knew what charges had been lodged against her. The police took her daughters to the house of a relative. The girls didn't know what happened to their mother until a year-and-a-half later.

For much of that time, Winnie was kept in solitary confinement at Pretoria Prison. During the first five months, she had no contact with anyone outside the walls of her prison. The light in her cell was kept on day and night. To keep her mind active, she unraveled one of the urine-stained blankets she had been given and carefully rewove it. Her desperation for the sight of something living caused her to search the cell for insects—an ant, a fly, anything else that was alive.

The worst thing for Winnie, always a scrupulously clean person, was the utter filth of the cell. Her diet of porridge and coffee, with an occasional scrap of unwashed, slimy spinach or a tough scrap of pork fat, took its toll on her body. She began to develop a skin infection due to a lack of vitamins.

After a time, the police began to interrogate her. She never knew what time of day it was or how long they questioned her. She fainted often, but the guards revived her, only to begin again. The chief interrogator warned her not to die until she had given the information that he wanted.

One day (it was July 18, 1969), the prison warden called Winnie to his office and asked who Thembi Mandela was. Winnie told him, "My son," for she had grown close to him and thought of him that way. Thembi had married, had two children, and sometimes visited Nelson in prison.

The warden told Winnie that Thembi had been killed in an automobile accident. Her first thought was of how this would affect Nelson.

Indeed, receiving the news of his eldest son's death was perhaps the hardest moment of Nelson's life in jail. He controlled his feelings long enough to return to his cell, and then wept. Of the three children Nelson had with Evelyn, Thembi had been hurt the most by his parents' divorce. But Nelson had high hopes for him. Now those were shattered. Nelson wrote to Thembi's widow and, for the first time, to Evelyn, his former wife.

After Winnie had spent two hundred days in jail, Nelson's lawyers finally obtained an order from the Supreme Court of South Africa easing her condition. For the first time she was allowed to take a shower. The chief interrogator appeared and flung a Bible, which she had requested, into her cell. He shouted: "There, pray in Xhosa, not in English!" She had irritated him by replying to his questions in English, not in his native Afrikaans.

Her trial proved to be an embarrassment for the government. Witness after witness told the judge that they had been tortured to force them to testify against Winnie. The attorney general announced he was abandoning the case, and the judge pronounced Winnie and those on trial with her not guilty of all charges. Among the things Winnie had been charged with were receiving instructions from a prisoner (Nelson) and reviving the outlawed ANC.

Incredibly, just after the judge's decision, the police arrived at the courtroom with machine guns and re-arrested all the prisoners. The whole process began again. Finally, at a second trial, in September 1970, a second judge acquitted them once more. The government promptly banned Winnie, preventing her from traveling to see Nelson.

During all this time, Mandela had had no letters from Winnie, and the letters he wrote her were never delivered. Except for Thembi, he didn't know what was happening to his children or how his wife was being treated. His feelings of helplessness and rage must have been great, but he never despaired.

Finally, Winnie obtained permission to visit Robben Island. She and Nelson had only half an hour to talk about what had happened in their lives during the past two years. Knowing this, Nelson prepared a written list of questions beforehand. A letter he wrote her later summed up his feelings about what she had suffered: "I am solidly behind you and know too well that you suffer because of your love and loyalty to the children and me, as well as to our large families. It is an ever-growing love and loyalty which strike me more forcefully every day you come."

8 A NAME THAT WOULD NOT DIE

The South African government believed that life imprisonment for Nelson Mandela would achieve two goals. The first was that his cause would be forgotten; the second, that it would break him as a man. Neither goal was achieved.

Indeed, Mandela's spirit was displayed in his response to a government proposal. The South African government was now carrying out its plan to give certain "Bantu" areas independence. Mandela's home area, the Transkei, was the first of these Bantustans, and his relative Kaiser Matanzima had accepted the government's offer of "independence." In December 1973 the Minister of Prisons offered Mandela his freedom after more than ten years in prison if he would agree to settle in the Transkei. This would encourage other black Africans to accept the policy of "separate development."

But Mandela would not trade his right to full citizenship in South Africa for freedom. He refused and continued to turn down similar offers each time they were made during his long years in prison.

BETTER CONDITIONS

Year by year, Mandela displayed his remarkable ability to master any situation in which he found himself, even the dreaded prison of Robben Island. In a letter to one of his biographers, he explained how he did it.

He wrote that the purpose of the prison was "to break the human spirit, to exploit human weakness, undermine human strength, destroy initiative, individuality [and] intelligence. . . . The great challenge is how to resist, how not to adjust . . . for that is the only way to maintain the human and the social within you."

The prison authorities sought to separate the prisoners from each other, to end human contact. "Locked up by yourself," Mandela wrote, "you came face to face with time and there is nothing more terrifying than to be alone with sheer time. Then the ghosts come crowding in . . . raising a thousand doubts in your mind about the people outside, their loyalty. Was your sacrifice worth the trouble? What would your life have been like if you hadn't got involved?"

Mandela found that to survive, every prisoner had to find his best talents and develop them. Some had talents with their minds, some with their hands. A fellow prisoner taught him mathematics and made a master key that could unlock any prison door. Others smuggled wood or stone into their cells and carved them into art.

At Robben Island, the prisoners created their own society, modeled after the one they hoped to establish outside prison. Committees were set up to encourage study, to keep discipline, to help prisoners who were losing faith in themselves and their cause. In the end, Mandela wrote, order in the prison was preserved not by the guards but by the prisoners.

The hard work the prisoners did was itself an antidote to boredom and declining spirits. Mandela now spent days on the beach collecting seaweed for fertilizer. From there, he could see ships in the distance heading for Cape Town. The sight reminded him that there was still a real world outside the confines of Robben Island. He told himself that someday he would rejoin that world.

In the 1970s, protests by international organizations won some concessions for the prisoners in Robben Island—more food, better blankets, and the right to talk to one another. Now they had hot water for washing and an outside volleyball court. Once a month they were permitted to play table tennis and chess and to see a movie.

After Mandela developed high blood pressure and a bad back, he was given a regular bed and better food. Winnie was permitted to visit him more frequently. His sister and his son Makgatho sometimes came with her. Yet the guards still listened to their conversations, interrupting them if Nelson asked about friends who were involved with political affairs.

Winnie noticed how Nelson had gradually assumed control of his situation. When a guard told them that time for the visit was up, Nelson spoke to him as if he were a child: "Surely you can see I'm in the middle of a sentence and haven't seen my family for some time. I'll continue anyhow, just continue listening, which is what your duty really is."

Mandela kept his deep commitment to educating himself. He took correspondence courses in law and economics, sending his examinations through the mail. He developed new interests in such subjects as archaeology, mythology, and religion. In a 1979 letter to Winnie, he said he felt guilty at being able to pursue his studies so easily while she had to struggle to further her own education in spite of government harassment.

"But remember," he wrote, "that I expect you to live up to the high standard I know you're capable of. But it really shook me to learn that in the evenings you drive to the public library. How can you take such a risk? Have you forgotten that you live in Soweto. . . . For the last decade you have been the subject of cowardly attempts on your life in which they tried to drag you out of the house. Your life and that of the children is more important than any educational certificate!"

The prison authorities found a new way to punish Nelson. The political prisoners were permitted to have paper only for study purposes and to write their twice-yearly letters. Now, in one of the regular searches of Mandela's tiny cell, the guards claimed to have found his "memoirs." Mandela demanded that the officials show the evidence, but they refused. As punishment, his rights to study were taken away for four years. He was not allowed to have any books or news from the outside, except for letters from Winnie.

THE SOWETO MASSACRE

Throughout the 1960s, virtually all the ANC leaders inside South Africa had been imprisoned. Late in the decade, as conditions worsened in the townships, a new movement arose, called Black Consciousness. Its spirit coincided with the black power movement in the United States, and had particularly great appeal for the young people. One of its leaders was Steve Biko.

Biko was a young student at the black University of Natal. Unlike Nelson, he had spent virtually his whole life under apartheid. Born in 1947, he had seen the government deny his people the right to a decent education, the freedom to protest peacefully, and any chance of attaining full rights. Biko and the other Black Consciousness leaders were attracted to the radical ideas of Robert Sobukwe and the PAC. They believed that black South Africans had to fight back on their own, without depending on white help.

In 1969, Biko helped form the all-black South African Students' Organization (SASO) to carry out the Black Consciousness program. Like Mandela and the other ANC firebrands who had created the Youth League, Biko and his associates wanted the country's restless, impatient young people to lead the way.

The "Bantu" schools, which were designed to educate blacks for nothing higher than manual labor, became a hotbed of support for the Black Consciousness movement. Teachers and students met secretly to plan how to carry on the struggle against the government.

In the early 1970s, the government announced that in the

Bantu schools some subjects would be taught only in Afrikaans. To the blacks, the language was that of their hated oppressors. Furthermore, by denying blacks knowledge of English, the government was attempting to further cut them off from the outside world. The combination of poor schooling, teaching in Afrikaans, and the growing militancy among young people created a political explosion.

In no part of the country was the Black Consciousness movement more popular than in Soweto. Soweto had grown over the years so that by the middle of the 1970s it was one of the biggest sub-Saharan African cities. A high proportion of the people living there were teenagers and children. The government announced its decision to build some decent housing there. As usual, this concession had a qualification: residents could own their little homes only if they accepted citizenship in their appropriate homelands. Knowing that this meant they could be evicted and deported at any time, most of the people refused.

During the years without Nelson, Winnie had grown both as a person and as a leader in the struggle for black rights. Living in Soweto, she was well aware of the growing militancy among its young people. Many parents came to her with their problems. They told her that children as young as eight were staying away from school to protest the new regulations. Many of the young people felt contempt for their parents, believing that they had not fought hard enough against the system.

The students soon began to organize a peaceful march to protest the use of Afrikaans in the schools. To give the lie to the government's charge that outside agitators were responsible for the protests, the students would wear school uniforms. The older students tried to exclude those of grade-school age from the march, but even the youngest wanted to be part of it.

Dr. Nthato Motlana, who had been Winnie's supervisor at the hospital years before, was now a leader in Soweto. He gave an eyewitness account of what happened in Soweto on June 16, 1976:

89

I saw a stream of schoolchildren marching past my house. . . . I followed them to see where they were going. . . . They had just reached the Orlando West school when the police tried to stop them [from] marching any further. The children kept on walking so the police released dogs. I did not see the pupils set upon the dogs but . . . later I saw a dead police dog that had been burnt. Then the police panicked and fired into the mass of children. . . . I will never forget the bravery of those children. They were carrying [trash can] lids to protect themselves and deflect the bullets. . . . The police had dogs and tear gas and batons, but they chose instead to use bullets against those unarmed kids. The saddest sight anyone can see is a dying child ripped by bullets.

That day, the guards on Robben Island were unusually harsh. Mandela sensed that something serious had happened. Though the day was rainy and cold, he and the others were forced to go outside to work. When they returned, there was no hot water in the showers—a petty punishment. But what caused it? He would not know for weeks.

Meanwhile, the government lost all control over Soweto. Protesters burned government buildings, schools, shops, post offices, and passing cars. More policemen arrived, but the violence continued for months.

A government report issued in 1977 put the number of dead at six hundred, although other estimates are that over one thousand died and some four thousand were wounded. Most of the dead were children. The police arrested countless others, including Winnie, Dr. Motlana, and other community leaders. They were held without charge or trial.

Some were tortured, including Steve Biko, who was interrogated for three weeks at the police headquarters in Port Elizabeth. Beaten nearly senseless, he was thrown naked into a police van and taken seven hundred miles to Pretoria Central Prison. He died the following day, September 12, 1977. Other leaders of Black Consciousness also died in custody, one by "falling" out of a tenth-story window in the headquarters of the Bureau of State Security (BOSS). (Seventy-four deaths occurred among jailed blacks in South Africa between 1963 and 1985.)

The world's newspapers condemned the killing of the children at Soweto. "Soweto" became a byword for brutality and injustice, but the South African government ignored international protests.

The violence radicalized the black youth of the townships of South Africa. In the years that followed, they took a leading role in the struggle against apartheid. Calling themselves the "comrades," these young people were more radical than any of the ANC leaders had been. In response to the brutal treatment of the government, they rejected nonviolence. They lashed out fiercely against any target they could find, including other blacks they suspected of cooperating with the government.

Mandela remained immured at Robben Island. But eventually the story of Soweto filtered through to him. He wrote Winnie a letter in which he described a beautiful tomato plant that he had been growing in the prison garden. He cared for it, watered it, and watched it grow with pride. But it was accidentally damaged and died. He told her how he dug it up and washed the soil off the roots, thinking of the fruit that it might have borne if it had lived.

Winnie understood. The story of the tomato plant was a parable. He could not describe his reaction to Soweto directly, for the prison officials would not send such a letter. Nelson's feelings about the tomato plant were those that swept through him when he heard about the children who died at Soweto.

Some of the young protestors arrested at Soweto were sentenced to go to Robben Island. One of the young prisoners recalled his arrival at the island. "The Boers brought us in, a bunch of us together on a boat, and I heard this voice, deep and strong, call out. . . . I looked up and there was Mandela." The young man's parents had warned him when he was a boy: "Don't get involved in politics. You'll end up like Mandela." Now that he had, he was immensely proud.

Mandela questioned them eagerly about everything that had happened on the outside. What was Black Consciousness? What did its followers believe? He listened attentively, sometimes nodding, sometimes frowning. He told one young man that the Black Consciousness followers were rash in their actions. The youngster laughed and said Mandela was just like his father. Finally, the young man recalled, Mandela agreed that "I was more radical than he was. Nelson did not argue against that."

Mandela had long sought to understand and learn from others. Now he became the teacher, convincing many of his new pupils that multi-racialism was a better policy than sheer hatred of whites. He pointed out that Black Consciousness was a state of mind that produced a desire to act. But it had no real plan of action other than anger. He began to train them, tell them what they must do when their sentences expired and they returned to the world outside prison. One of his pupils called Robben Island "Mandela University."

The prison authorities separated some of the youngest prisoners from the others. But they too wanted to see Mandela. They began to leave messages at the iron gate that separated their exercise yard from his. They asked that he stand where they could see him at a certain time. "He did as we requested," one recalled, "and we saw him standing, tall, slim, very regal. We did not speak, and we made no signs, we looked in wonder at the man and, later, we talked about him with excitement."

Meanwhile, Mandela received word that Winnie had been released from detention in the Soweto roundup. But four months later, the government banned her to a distant part of the country. Brandfort was a small town in the flat veld of the Orange Free State. The government felt that by sending her there it could prevent her from influencing public opinion. As a banned person, she could not speak in public, nor could any statement by her appear in South African newspapers.

However, foreign journalists soon began coming to her little house in Brandfort. They could print what she said, and she continually reminded the world that Nelson Mandela was still in prison, still suffering for demanding the rights of his people. Foreign diplomats, such as the German ambassador to South Africa, also came to see her. The world would not forget.

Mandela received another letter from Winnie, telling him that their older daughter, Zeni, had gotten married. Her husband was one of the sons of the king of Swaziland. Winnie had to battle for permission to leave the country, but she succeeded in attending her daughter's traditional marriage ceremony. Mandela, of course, could not leave prison, and he missed another milestone of his family's life.

SIXTIETH BIRTHDAY

Mandela once wrote Winnie that without her letters and visits and her love, "I would have fallen apart many years ago." As part of his daily routine, he dusted her photograph, which stood on a shelf in his cell between pictures of Zeni and Zindzi.

In June 1978, Zeni brought her husband and year-old daughter to visit Nelson. As the wife of a Swaziland prince, she used her diplomatic privilege to arrange the meeting. For the first time in his prison life, Mandela was allowed to see visitors in person, not through a glass window.

He had not seen a baby for sixteen years, and as he entered the visitors' room, Zeni placed his own grandchild in his arms. He was so moved that Zeni thought he would break down. She told herself not to cry so that he wouldn't either. He and Zeni held each other for a long time. Not in all the time he had been in prison had he actually touched another member of his family.

Zeni and her husband had waited to meet Nelson before naming the baby. To do that would be his honor, and he called her Zaziwe, or "Hope."

Meeting Zeni was like a birthday present, for a month later Nelson celebrated his sixtieth birthday. The occasion brought tributes from governments and international organizations around the world. Thousands of people who knew him only as a legend sent birthday cards to South Africa. But he could not see a single one, for the prison refused to let him receive them. Instead, they were delivered to Winnie's house in Brandfort.

Certainly, the tribute dearest to his heart had to be a poem written by his younger daughter Zindzi:

> *A tree was chopped down*
> *and the fruit was scattered*
> *I cried*
> *because I had lost a family*
> *the trunk, my father*
> *the branches, his support*
> *so much*
> *the fruit, the wife and children*
> *who meant so much to him*
> *tasty*
> *loving as they should be*
> *all on the ground*
> *some out of his reach*
> *in the ground*
> *the roots, happiness*
> *cut off from him.*

Nelson wrote to Zindzi, describing his thoughts in prison. His letters show that he had overcome the brutality and cruelty he met with daily. His serenity and inner strength could not be defeated.

"On some days," he wrote,

> *the weather on the island is quite beautiful. . . . Early one morning, I looked out through the window and the eye could see eastwards as far as the distant horizon. The power of imagination created the illusion that my vision went much farther than the naked eye could actually see. I could survey vast regions behind the long mountain ranges where I have never been. Later, I walked out into the courtyard*

and the few living things there, the seagulls, wagtails, the plants, small trees and even grass blades were gay and full of smiles. Everything was caught up in the beauty of the day.

They could imprison his body, but his spirit soared free.

9 FREE MANDELA!

During the 1970s and 1980s, Nelson Mandela became the most famous political prisoner in the world. Awards from many nations showered down on him. In 1979, he was awarded the Nehru Prize, India's highest honor. This was very meaningful to him because of the role of Gandhi's ideas in South Africa. Zeni went to accept it for him, and brought him an album of photographs of the ceremony.

Universities in Belgium, England, and Philadelphia awarded Mandela honorary degrees. The city of London honored him with a bronze statue; at its base were the words he had made famous: "The Struggle Is My Life." Other towns and cities named streets and parks in his honor. In the early 1980s, a petition demanding his freedom was sent to South Africa's government. It had been signed by two thousand mayors of cities in fifty-three countries.

The "Free Mandela" movement grew particularly popular among young people. A British rock group made a record titled "Free Nelson Mandela." Teenagers wore T-shirts with his picture—a photograph that had been taken many years before. No one except those who visited him knew what he actually looked like, for the government resolutely forbade anyone to photograph him. South Africa's apartheid regime still hoped that Nelson would be forgotten, but by now that was impossible.

At home, the name Nelson Mandela became a rallying cry for protesters—some of whom were not yet born when Nelson went to prison. In the night, people painted his name on the walls of buildings. "Mandela" meant resistance, pride, and hope. Though it was illegal even to quote Mandela in the country, he assumed mythic proportions among the majority of South Africa's blacks.

LEAVING ROBBEN ISLAND

Pressure from groups at home and abroad caused the government to ease its treatment of Mandela and the other political prisoners. The prisoners could now receive two newspapers every day. Mandela was delighted, for at last he could keep in touch with what was going on in the outside world. Moreover, the political prisoners were no longer required to do hard labor. They could sell the produce from their small gardens and buy extra food and other items from the prison commissary.

In 1982, in the middle of the night, Mandela, Sisulu, and three others sentenced at the Rivonia trial were awakened by the guards. They were taken in a boat to the mainland and driven to Pollsmoor Prison, an hour away from Cape Town. Newspaper stories about the horrors of Robben Island had caused the government to shift them to a new prison.

Pollsmoor was a modern facility with thousands of other prisoners, but all were segregated according to South Africa's complex racial system. Life here was in some ways better. Friends from Cape Town could bring meals for the prisoners. Nelson and the others could use the library, which had foreign publications, and listen to the radio.

The guards also seemed less brutal than those at Robben Island. Mandela became friendly with an English-speaking guard, who treated Winnie and Zeni courteously when they came to visit. Though they still sat on either side of a window, they could see and hear each other more clearly than they had at Robben Island.

The government had another reason for shifting Mandela out of Robben Island. It had seen the effect he was having on the younger prisoners. Now Mandela and his old friends were isolated on the third floor of a building. When they went outside, they were carefully supervised. He missed his garden and the walks along the seashore. Unlike Robben Island, nothing grew at Pollsmoor, not even a blade of grass.

When rains came, the water seeped through the walls of the dormitory where Mandela, Sisulu, and four other men lived. Mandela had been given shoes that were too small for him, and with the dampness, he developed an infected toe. Eventually, he had to have an operation. He told Winnie that his health was deteriorating. She was alarmed, for he had never complained about his personal discomfort before.

When Winnie made the matter public, the government made another concession. On her next visit, the guard told her that Mandela was now allowed "contact" visits. On May 12, 1984, for the first time in twenty-two years, he and Winnie met without a pane of glass between them. They kissed and held each other, thinking of the years they had lost.

CHANGES IN APARTHEID

Conditions outside the prison were not improving. The young "comrades" in the townships now carried on the fight, and the government found them more radical than the older generation had been. Furthermore, protests in other countries caused some international businesses to pressure the government to ease its policies.

In 1983, the government tried to divide the opposition by announcing plans to write a new constitution. It would allow the country's colored and Asian people to elect their own representatives, but they would serve in parliaments separate from the white one. The vast majority of South Africans—the blacks—would still have no representation.

98

An election was held to decide whether to adopt the new constitution; only whites were allowed to vote. Some ultra-nationalist white groups opposed even this concession to non-whites and formed their own political party in protest. But the new constitution was approved.

The government thought that its new offer would cause coloreds and Asians to abandon the movement advocating rights for all. But it backfired. A new, more widely based opposition group arose. The United Democratic Front (UDF) was formed in 1983 to oppose the new constitution. It included approximately four hundred separate organizations—black, white, colored, and Asian. Trade unions, church groups, and student organizations all sent representatives to the first UDF conference. Winnie became a member, and Nelson managed to smuggle a message of solidarity out of the prison to be read to the delegates. Other supporters included the colored leader Dr. Allan Boesak and the black church leader Bishop Desmond Tutu, who was later to win the Nobel Peace Prize.

The year after the constitution was approved, elections were held for the new parliaments. The UDF called for a boycott of the elections. Contrary to government expectations, the voting turnout was low. The new parliaments were seen for what they were: window dressing. Their decisions could be overruled by the white parliament.

Blacks in the townships opposed the new constitution in the only way open to them—they threw stones at police. The police fired back with rifles. Each time they killed someone, the township staged a huge funeral procession, and police arrived to continue the cycle of violence.

In their rage, blacks in the townships turned on each other. Those who were thought to be police informers or collaborators were attacked and killed by other blacks. A particularly gruesome method of executing traitors was called "necklacing." A rubber tire was soaked in gasoline, thrown around the neck of the victim, and set afire. Black leaders like Bishop Tutu went to the townships to stop black-on-black violence, but they were helpless to control the anger of their people.

Television crews from around the world recorded the sight of security police beating and killing blacks armed with stones. The international protest that followed caused the South African government to declare a state of emergency in 1985. Reporters and their cameras were barred from entering areas where disturbances occurred. All they could do was report the casualty statistics released by the government.

Security police moved through the townships, arresting anyone suspected of anti-apartheid activities. Thousands of people were detained. During 1985 alone, the police arrested 2,106 children under the age of sixteen.

Overseas, people were revolted by the government's brutal treatment of the black population. They wanted to do something to help, and the only way seemed to be hitting South Africa in the pocketbook. For years the ANC in exile had called for economic sanctions, or a cutback in trade with South Africa. Now overseas organizations took up the idea, and it rapidly gained acceptance.

These economic sanctions took two forms. One was disinvestment—multinational corporations were urged to close their offices and factories in South Africa. Another was divestiture—selling shares of stock in all companies that did business in South Africa.

Groups in the United States (and other countries) proposed boycotts against companies that did business with South Africa. They pressured American businesses with interests in the country to withdraw their economic cooperation. Union pension plans, universities, insurance companies, and other large stockholders began to sell stock in companies that dealt with South Africa. In 1986, the U.S. Congress passed an economic sanctions law that restricted trade and business between the two countries.

Not everyone agreed that sanctions were the best way to combat apartheid. Many of South Africa's black workers were

100

employed by branches of overseas companies. Thus, they would be the first ones hurt by these companies pulling out.

One black South African leader who opposed sanctions was Mangosuthu Gatsha Buthelezi. Buthelezi was descended from a Zulu royal family. As a young man he had been a member of the ANC. But in 1970 he had accepted the government's appointment as the leader of KwaZulu, one of the independent "homelands" that Mandela and the ANC opposed. When other black leaders condemned him, Buthelezi formed his own Zulu rights organization, called Inkatha. He criticized the UDF for advocating sanctions and anti-government demonstrations.

In the eyes of some, Buthelezi was a traitor for cooperating with the government. In his own defense, he argued, "There was no choice for me." He took what the government offered because it was a step toward full rights. He opposed sanctions because they would hurt blacks most of all. But violence between Zulu members of Inkatha and other blacks broke out, and has continued to the present day.

And so the struggle went on. The illegal ANC flag was draped over the coffins of men, women, and children who had been killed by government police who dared to enter black areas only in armored cars. Mandela in prison was only a symbol that the nation itself was a prison for blacks.

MANDELA'S INFLUENCE

In January 1985, South Africa's President Pieter W. Botha announced that the government would be willing to release Mandela if he agreed to renounce violence unconditionally. Winnie and her lawyer came to Pollsmoor to get Nelson's response.

He dictated a message that his daughter Zindzi read to a UDF gathering in Soweto on February 10: "My father says, 'I am surprised at the conditions that the government wants to impose on me. I am not a violent man. My colleagues and I wrote in 1952 to Malan [Daniel Malan, then prime minister] asking for a round table conference to find a solution to the problems of our country but that was ignored.'"

He recounted the offers that the ANC had made to succeeding governments. All had been ignored.

> *It was only then when all other forms of resistance were no longer open to us that we turned to armed struggle. Let Botha show that he is different. . . . Let him renounce violence. Let him say that he will dismantle apartheid. Let him unban the people's organization, the African National Congress. Let him free all who have been imprisoned, banished or exiled for their opposition to apartheid. Let him guarantee free political activity so that the people may decide who will govern them.*
>
> *I cherish my own freedom dearly but I care even more for your freedom. Too many have died since I went to prison. . . . Not only I have suffered during these long lonely wasted years. I am not less life-loving than you are. But I cannot sell my birthright . . . to be free. . . . What freedom am I being offered when I need a stamp in my pass to seek work? What freedom am I being offered when my very South African citizenship is not respected?*
>
> *Only free men can negotiate. Prisoners cannot enter into contracts. . . . I cannot and will not give any undertaking at a time when I and you, the people, are not free. Your freedom and mine cannot be separated. I will return.*

Protests from overseas forced the government to allow foreign visitors to see Nelson in prison. One of them was the American lawyer Samuel Dash. Like other visitors, Dash noted that Nelson seemed to act as though he were the superior, not the prisoner, of the guards who accompanied him. Dressed in neatly pressed, immaculate clothing, Mandela quietly directed the guards to open gates and unlock doors as he took Dash on a tour of the prison.

Mandela explained to Dash the three principles of the ANC program: (1) a unified South Africa without artificial "homelands," (2) black representation in the central parliament, and (3) "one person, one vote."

Dash pointed out that many whites feared that if these demands were granted, blacks would take over the country and expel the whites. Nelson said that these fears were groundless. "Unlike white people anywhere else in Africa," Mandela said, "whites in South Africa belong here—this is their home. We want them to live here with us and to share power with us."

SORROW AND HOPE

While Nelson was preparing his response to Botha's offer, he heard that one of Winnie's sisters had died. Moved by sadness and guilt over the life he had made for Winnie, he wrote to her:

> *On occasions like this I often wonder just how far more difficult it would have been for me to take the decision to leave you behind if I had been able to see clearly the countless perils and hardships to which you would be exposed in my absence. . . .*
>
> *Your love and support . . . the charming children you have given the family, the many friends you have won, the hope of enjoying that love and warmth again, is what life and happiness mean to me. . . .*
>
> *Yet there have been moments when that love and happiness . . . have turned into pure agony, when conscience and a sense of guilt have ravaged every part of my being, when I have wondered whether any kind of commitment can ever be sufficient excuse for abandoning a young and inexperienced woman in a pitiless desert . . . a wonderful woman without her pillar and support at times of need.*

His fears were justified, for Winnie now entered a phase of her life in which she would need Nelson more than ever. Late in 1985, she moved back to Soweto, where she threw herself into active political work.

103

In Soweto, Winnie saw violence virtually every day. Police in armored cars and soldiers in tanks patrolled the streets. The young militant blacks known as the "comrades" openly defied them. Clashes often resulted.

In the Xhosa language, the comrades called themselves *amadla kufa,* the defiers of death. They were literally fearless, and would stop at nothing to win freedom. In addition, they regarded any blacks who cooperated with the government as traitors, and used the fiery "necklaces" to punish them.

In Soweto, the world of the comrades became Winnie's world. She exulted in the title they gave her, *Umama Wethu,* "mother of the nation." Her public speeches became more radical, and sometimes she espoused violence. In 1986, she declared, "Together, hand in hand, with our boxes of matches and necklaces we shall liberate this country." The exiled ANC leadership repudiated this remark, the first time it had ever split with Winnie.

But worse things were to come. Winnie's home at 8115 Orlando became the headquarters of a group of young men called the Mandela Football Club. They served as her bodyguards, and wherever she went, the shouting, dancing club members accompanied her. The club bullied and threatened other residents of Soweto, creating hostility. Police were often called to break up fights between neighbors and club members in the yard of Winnie's home.

Rumors grew about the sinister activities of the club. Its members were said to have killed "collaborators." They carved the letters ANC or M into the skin of youths who criticized them. It was reported that the penalty for trying to leave the club was execution.

The Soweto community protested the club's violence, but when leaders of the community tried to meet with Winnie, she did not show up. In 1988, her home was burned to the ground while she was away. None of Winnie's neighbors attempted to put the fire out. From Pollsmoor, Nelson sent word that he did not wish to see anyone punished for the arson. Friends had already warned him that Winnie's association with the club was dangerous.

Then came the incident that created headlines around the world. The club members abducted four young men who were staying in a shelter run by a white minister. They brought them to Winnie's new house and accused them of being government informers. When the young men denied it, club members—and, allegedly, Winnie herself—beat them with whips and fists.

One of the four prisoners was a fourteen-year-old boy named James (Stompie) Moeketsi Seipei. Stompie was already a famous veteran of the antiapartheid movement. At age eleven, he had organized a children's army in his home area in the Orange Free State. The government had detained him in jail for a year. After his release, he spoke to a mass meeting at Witwatersrand University, reading from the Freedom Charter. Recently, the security police had arrested him again, torturing him to force him to give information about the movement. The club members claimed that he had talked and must be punished.

The four were detained in Winnie's house for three days. The others saw that Stompie was severely injured and in need of medical help. The "coach" of the Football Club took him away. Stompie's body was later found in a field.

As the ugly story spread, people who had long admired Winnie wanted to know: How could this happen? She had devoted herself to medical social work and had helped children throughout her career. But since 1962, when Nelson went to prison, she had faced a life of bannings, imprisonment, and constant harassment. The pluck and defiance she had shown toward police and guards hardened into hatred. Living among the "comrades," she had adopted their attitude that anyone who betrayed the struggle was a traitor. Perhaps too, the international adulation had gone to her head, making her feel that anything she did was justified.

Winnie claimed that she was innocent of any involvement in Stompie's death. Nelson believed Winnie's denials; he could not bear to think otherwise. For over twenty years she had been his link to the outside world. Her letters and love were all that made his imprisonment endurable. His loyalty to her could never be shaken. He accused the government of "most scandalous persecution" of Winnie.

A TEA PARTY WITH THE PRESIDENT

At this time, Nelson was suffering from a serious illness. When Winnie and Zindzi visited him, they found that he had lost a great deal of weight. His face was wrinkled and looked old. A doctor diagnosed his illness as tuberculosis, but said that with treatment he would recover. He was taken to a hospital. Some thought that his anxiety over Winnie's activities had brought on the illness.

But in the hospital, Mandela gradually improved and began to look more like his old self. He resumed his morning push-up exercises. The government, worried that a new wave of protests would begin if he died in jail, announced that he would not return to Pollsmoor. In December 1988, he was taken to Victor Verster Prison, a minimum-security facility. There he lived alone in a three-bedroom house; the government said his family could visit at any time and even live there.

Nelson decided that Winnie should not move in with him. He refused because his comrades in Pollsmoor and Robben Island were allowed no such privileges. Until all of them were free, he would not allow himself to be freed. He had turned the tables on the government—though it wanted to release him, he would negotiate the terms of his own freedom.

When Winnie came to him, they discussed the Football Club. She disbanded it and followed his advice not to give interviews to the press. One of his old friends wrote, "Those who visited him at this time saw his distress . . . and his unswerving love for his wife."

Seven months after Nelson moved into his new prison, he received a startling invitation. President P. W. Botha asked

106

Nelson Mandela, the dangerous "traitor" serving life in prison, to come to his house for tea. Nelson graciously accepted.

The leader of white South Africa and the legendary opponent of apartheid spoke in private for forty-five minutes. Neither gave any indication of what had been said. Afterward, Nelson commented, "I only would like to contribute to the creation of a climate which would promote peace in South Africa."

But others spoke out. Many South Africans of all races were relieved that at last the two sides were approaching some kind of agreement. They hoped for an end to the bitter hatred between the races. But some white Africans termed Botha a traitor. The ruling National party was not the most extreme group in the country. Other parties, some styling themselves after Hitler's Nazi party, wanted to preserve and even extend white supremacy. On the other hand, some blacks complained that Mandela should not meet with Botha until the government ended its ban on the ANC and freed all political prisoners.

From prison, Mandela responded to his critics by saying that dialogue with the government was "the only way of ending violence and bringing peace." Over seventy years old now, Mandela wanted to see a united and free South Africa before he died. The government encouraged further talks by saying it would consider writing a new constitution. Anyone who "had a commitment to peace" would be welcome to take part in discussions for a new South Africa.

The first step had been taken. The only question now was, how far was South Africa's government prepared to go?

10 FREEDOM

Hopes that President Botha might free Nelson Mandela were dashed when Botha suffered a stroke in January 1989. Frederik Willem de Klerk became the leader of the National party, which had controlled the South African government since 1948. Although Botha clung to the presidency until August, de Klerk was now his certain successor.

De Klerk had held many party and government posts, but no one knew his real feelings about the issues that the country faced. When he became head of the National Party, the London *Observer* called him "the man with the perfect resume, but no footprints." At times he appeared to favor the hardliners, as when he criticized Botha for meeting with Mandela. On the other hand, he had spoken of the need for reform to avoid national disaster.

De Klerk's ancestors had been active in South African politics for many generations. The De Klerk family reflected a range of Afrikaner opinions—some were enlightened, others reactionary. When Frederik was twelve, his father, Jan, played an important role in the National party's victory of 1948. His uncle, Johannes Strijdom, was prime minister of the country in the 1950s. Young Frederik gained a love for politics and a deep attachment to the National party, which had carried out the apartheid program.

His mother, however, had a gentler vision and more liberal views, which influenced Frederik's older brother Willem, a newspaper editor. Through his strong religious beliefs, Willem came to believe that apartheid was "not founded in morality." He began to write and speak out against apartheid and committed what Afrikaners regarded as a treasonous act—he held discussions with the leaders of the outlawed ANC.

In contrast, Frederik appeared a conformist, the ultimate party man, dedicated to the system. Still, on assuming party leadership, Frederik stated, "White domination, insofar as it exists, must go." The statement appeared to be a half-step forward. It did not prepare South Africa for the sweeping changes that de Klerk would soon propose.

After becoming president in August, de Klerk quickly showed the direction he intended to follow. On October 15, Walter Sisulu and other Rivonia prisoners were released from jail. There was only one left—Nelson Mandela.

A joyous crowd, waving the banned ANC flag, welcomed Sisulu and the other ex-prisoners to Soweto. Sisulu urged them to keep their celebration peaceful. The government might well have released him and the others as a test of public opinion. Some whites had long feared that if Mandela were freed, it would set off a wave of violence that would lead to open revolution.

Sisulu asked the black Africans in the townships to be patient. He advised them to organize peacefully and wait for talks with the government to begin. He called for an end to the violence that still wracked Soweto and other townships.

In January 1990, Sisulu met in Zambia with the exiled leaders of the ANC. The ANC declared its willingness to engage in peaceful negotiations with the South African government. This gave the government the confidence to move forward.

On February 2, President de Klerk addressed the South African Parliament in Cape Town. "The season of violence is

109

over," he declared. "The time for reconciliations and reconstruction has arrived." To back up his words, he ended the ban on outlawed antiapartheid organizations, including the ANC, the PAC, and the Communist party. He lifted most of the restrictions on the press and media, freed other nonviolent political prisoners, and suspended executions. And he promised that Mandela would be freed—without conditions. His speech and actions raised hopes throughout the country and the world.

FREE AT LAST

On February 11, 1990, the sun shone in a clear blue sky over Victor Verster Prison. Television crews and reporters from around the world were waiting to record the release of the world's most famous political prisoner. Since before dawn, a crowd of people had been gathering at the prison gate. The excitement was electric.

Virtually no pictures of Mandela had been taken since he had entered prison twenty-seven years ago. Then, he had been a big burly man, powerful and youthful. What would he look like now? Restless anticipation stirred the crowd.

Finally, just after four o'clock in the afternoon, the crowd saw a tall, silver-haired man wearing a dark suit approaching the gates. They knew who it was, for Winnie was next to him. Hand in hand, they walked through the prison gates. Nelson looked up at the sky, savoring the limitless freedom that he had imagined for so long. Then he focused his eyes on the people gathered around, almost as if he were surprised to see them. He smiled and raised a clenched fist.

He spoke no words; none were necessary, for all shared the feeling of sheer delight that the day of freedom had come at last. Mandela himself had sometimes doubted that he would ever see it. As he stood there under the hot African sun, the people cheered till their throats were raw.

Mandela got into a waiting car and it drove off, headed for Cape Town, where he was scheduled to give a speech. But he carried a burden with him—the hopes of 27 million black

South Africans and indeed of many others who knew that South Africa's best chance for peace rested on this man's shoulders.

Motorcycle police (who asked Mandela for his autograph) escorted his car on the road to Cape Town. The route was lined with cheering supporters, both white and black. Fighting broke out among those who tried to push forward, and police fired into the crowd. Mandela may have been free, but South Africa still was not.

Meanwhile, more than fifty thousand people waited to greet him in Cape Town. When the motorcade fell behind schedule, the crowd grew restless. The committee that had prepared this welcoming celebration had provided few security guards, thinking that they were unnecessary. But young black toughs started fights and destroyed the platform for the TV crews. People began to leave, and by the time Mandela finally arrived, the crowd was down to ten thousand. It was not a good beginning and was typical of the problems Nelson would face.

When Mandela finally rose to speak, he thanked all those who had stood by him in the struggle. He promised to be "a humble servant of you, the people. I . . . place the remaining years of my life in your hands."

What the world saw was a vigorous seventy-one-year-old man of great dignity. He had emerged from twenty-seven years in prison with a singular lack of bitterness. The heavyset, youthful revolutionary had been transformed into a slim, silver-haired statesman.

Mandela's return to Soweto two days later went much more smoothly. The rally to welcome him home was held in the Soccer City Stadium and one hundred thousand people attended. This time security conditions were better. The South African Youth Congress provided volunteers. Arriving by helicopter, Mandela, Sisulu, their wives, and other ANC leaders acknowledged the cheers of the crowd. All eyes were on Nelson. The crowd chanted, "Viva Mandela!" and "ANC, ANC" over and over. Walter Sisulu made an opening speech, and then the crowd went wild as Mandela went to the microphone.

It took fifteen minutes for the cheers to die down enough to allow him to speak. He seemed to have the "comrades" on his mind. Many of them had abandoned their education in protest against the government's policies. He urged the youths to return to school, and he spoke out against black violence against other blacks. "The hijacking and setting alight of vehicles and harassment of innocent people are criminal acts which have no place in our struggle," he declared. In particular, he called for an end to "mindless violence" in Natal, where fighting had taken place between Buthelezi's Inkatha movement and supporters of the ANC.

When he finished, hundreds of black, green, and gold balloons rose into the air and dancers dressed in the ANC colors paraded across the field. The crowd stood as Mandela's helicopter rose into the air, taking him to his house in Soweto.

For the first time in twenty-seven years, Mandela could enjoy his family. He played with his grandchildren and welcomed old friends and relatives who came by the house. It could not have been easy to adjust to daily life in a world that had changed greatly since he last lived free.

But there was little time to rest. He was faced with a unique opportunity. He was the hero of the moment. No other South African had his international prestige. No other leader could command the respect of so many of the blacks of South Africa. Yet the great challenge was how to use this popularity.

President de Klerk had visited Mandela before releasing him from prison. The two had established a good personal relationship. But de Klerk was not entirely free to make the changes that were necessary to bring about a new form of government. Many members of his own National party opposed concessions to the black majority, and the Nationalists were moderate compared to other groups. The right-wing Conservative party, which held forty-one seats in the nation's parliament, openly favored continued white supremacy and strict apartheid laws. De Klerk did not have to call new elections until 1994, but some paramilitary white groups threatened violent resistance to any concessions to Mandela and the ANC.

112

Members of the Afrikaner Resistance Movement marched through Pretoria, shouting, "Hang de Klerk, hang Mandela!"

Furthermore, Mandela himself had to live up to the enormous expectations his release had created among blacks. For years, not only whites but blacks had believed that once Mandela was free, blacks would virtually take over the country. That could not happen immediately without horrendous bloodshed, which Mandela was determined to avoid. But if time went by and no tangible signs of progress appeared, blacks would become disillusioned. The "comrades" might become increasingly violent, and other leaders, like Buthelezi, would challenge Nelson's authority.

Mandela also had to unite different factions within the ANC. It had to be transformed from a guerrilla exile group into a political party. Now that it was free to operate, the ANC faced the difficult task of developing a practical program that took South Africa's political realities into account. Besides Buthelezi's Inkatha, many other grass-roots organizations had arisen to take the place of the banned ANC. How would their leaders and members respond to the ANC's attempt to unite all of them into a single, powerful force?

Mandela went to the city of Durban and spoke to another huge crowd. He urged all to unite to stop the violence. "Take your guns, your knives and your *pangas* [machetes] and throw them into the sea," he told them. He held out a hand of conciliation, saying, "We have reached a stage where none of the parties can be regarded as right or wrong."

Then he was off to Zambia, where he met the ANC's exiled leaders. They held five days of talks, deciding what the future course of the ANC should be. The ANC appointed Mandela as its deputy president. Since Oliver Tambo, the longtime president, was disabled by a stroke, this meant that Mandela was the effective head of the organization. He was also named to lead a delegation to begin talks with de Klerk about solutions to the country's many problems.

Mandela continued on a triumphal tour of Africa, visiting Zimbabwe, Tanzania, and Ethiopia in March. All three nations had allowed the ANC to set up training camps, schools, and farms for black South Africans who had fled the country. On March 12, Mandela went to Sweden, where his old law partner, Oliver Tambo, was recuperating from a stroke. For the first time in nearly twenty-eight years, Tambo and Mandela were reunited. The old friends had many memories to catch up on together. But their time was all too short. There was too much to do.

De Klerk announced that talks with Mandela and the ANC would begin on April 11. But on March 26, police fired on antiapartheid demonstrators in Sebokeng township, south of Johannesburg. The protesters were trying to deliver a petition to the local police station. In the attack, eleven people were killed and over one hundred wounded. Mandela was outraged at the slaughter, and the talks were suspended.

He met with de Klerk, who assured him that the police would be controlled. A new date for the talks was set. On May 2, de Klerk and Mandela appeared together in public for the first time. Outside Groote Schuur, a Dutch-style mansion in suburban Cape Town, Mandela said, "This is the first time in 78 years that a truly serious meeting takes place between delegations of the African National Congress and the . . . white governments that have ruled our country for generations. This . . . indicates the deadly weight of the terrible tradition of a dialogue between master and servant which we have to overcome."

The talks were only a preliminary to the hard bargaining that both sides knew would follow. The ANC demanded that the government end the current state of emergency, free all political prisoners, and allow those in exile to return. The government responded by insisting that the ANC renounce its commitment to armed struggle and use its influence to stop the violence that had spread throughout the townships.

As for a new form of government, the ANC wanted one-person, one-vote majority rule, with an end to the separate homelands. De Klerk opposed such a change, which most whites feared would lead to black domination. He offered a decentralized form of government that would enable any minority group to veto proposals affecting its communities. Whites would thus be protected.

The talks ended with minor agreements regarding the release of political prisoners. The government promised to review existing security laws, and the ANC pledged to work to bring about peace and stability.

Both sides would have to convince their supporters of the wisdom of the changes being contemplated. All the members of the right-wing Conservative party had walked out of Parliament to protest the talks. When the ANC tried to organize a meeting of the six homeland leaders, Chief Buthelezi refused to attend. Members of his Inkatha group had already fought violent battles with supporters of the ANC in Natal province. The road to peace appeared to be a long one.

THE GRAND TOUR

Mandela's doctors were worried about the pace that he was setting for himself. Dozens of organizations in many countries were inviting him to visit, and he seemed inclined to accept virtually all invitations. A seventy-two-year-old man who had just emerged from nearly three decades in prison could not possibly endure this kind of activity—or so the doctors thought.

That summer, Mandela set off on a six-week world tour that would take him to fourteen countries. He had two main goals for his grueling trip. First, he wanted to use his personal prestige to urge foreign governments to keep up the economic sanctions on South Africa. In addition, Mandela used his tour as a fund-raising trip. The ANC needed money to carry on the necessary work of organizing blacks into a legitimate, powerful political party.

Mandela arrived in the United States on June 20. New York, the first city he visited, was charmed and thrilled by his appearance. At the airport, David Dinkins, New York's first black mayor, along with the governors of New York and New

Jersey, were among the many politicians and celebrities who virtually pushed to get beside him for the TV cameras.

For many African Americans, his visit was a high point of their lives. A delivery man who did not get to see Mandela in the crush of people expressed his feelings: "I saw Mandela in my heart, and he touched my heart more than any [other] individual. This moment summed up the feelings of a lifetime."

Behind the scenes, Mandela was feeling his age. He arrived two hours late for a reception because he needed time to rest. But the cheering throngs seemed to rejuvenate him, and he spoke with a voice that was strong and determined.

Significantly, Mandela's first stop in New York was at a school in Bedford-Stuyvesant, a black ghetto area of Brooklyn. He asked the cheering students to support South African children, who lacked such ordinary school supplies as pencils, paper, and books.

Then Nelson and Winnie were treated to a ticker-tape parade on Broadway—the welcome that the Big Apple traditionally gives its most honored guests. For security's sake they rode in a bulletproof glass box on top of a flatbed truck. The media dubbed it "the Mandela-mobile." Three quarters of a million people lined the route.

More were waiting at City Hall, where Mayor Dinkins gave Mandela the key to the city. Standing on the steps outside the building, Mandela urged the crowd to "Keep the Pressure On." This was the theme of his trip—don't stop the sanctions on South Africa just because Mandela was free. All South Africa must be free.

At Manhattan's Riverside Church, Mandela roused his followers with a stirring speech. The celebrants were dancing in the aisles. Mandela quoted from the Book of Isaiah: "We have risen up on the wings of eagles."

That evening, Yankee Stadium was packed with those who wanted to see and hear him. He thanked his followers for supporting him throughout the long years in prison. "From behind the granite walls, political prisoners could hear loud and clear your voice of solidarity. . . . We are winning because you made it possible." The mayor slipped a New York Yankees team jacket onto Mandela's shoulders. Smiling, Mandela stepped forward to display the gift and announced, "Now I am a Yankee."

Day after day, he continued his public appearances. The most jubilant response came in Harlem, where African-American culture had flowered during the 1920s. Mandela stood and invoked the heroes of Black America—Martin Luther King, Jr., Malcolm X, and Paul Robeson, among others. "I am here to claim you because . . . you have claimed our struggle," Mandela told the cheering throng. "Harlem signifies the glory of resistance. We are on the verge of victory." The crowd's loudest cheers came when Mandela shouted, "Death to racism!"

The tour continued to other cities. In Boston, Mandela visited the John F. Kennedy Library. In Washington, D.C., he spoke before Congress and then visited the White House for private talks with President George Bush. As vice president, Bush had discouraged U.S. economic sanctions against South Africa. But now he promised to wait until the South African government made reforms before lifting them.

In a stop in Atlanta, Mandela laid a wreath on the grave of Martin Luther King, Jr. Farther south, in Miami, he encountered criticism. Mandela had earlier praised Fidel Castro, Yasir Arafat, and Muammar Khaddafi for their support of the ANC. Some Americans saw these leaders as deadly enemies, and in Miami the mayor refused to meet Mandela.

Mandela went on to Detroit, where he spoke to a group of automobile workers. He came to thank them, for their union was among the first groups to call for sanctions against South Africa. He also attended a concert that featured the "Motown sound." Reporters asked what he thought about the music. He told them that he had often enjoyed it, for even in a South African prison, the records of Motown groups were played on the radio.

He wound up his American trip in California, where he met a host of celebrities who wrote generous checks for the

ANC. Mandela recalled how much he had loved Hollywood movies as a young man. He had been inspired and encouraged by their images of a freer, more open society.

The tour had been a triumph in many ways. Mandela had raised money and increased support for his cause. He had met with prominent business and banking leaders to discuss investment in the new South Africa that he hoped would arise. He promised that the ANC would not totally oppose a free-market economy. He said he wanted South Africa to prosper, for black Africans would finally share in the country's wealth.

On a personal level, standing before multitudes of cheering people had boosted the spirits of both Nelson and Winnie. Winnie later said, "I don't think I can translate into words that warmth. . . . We were overwhelmed. I don't think we'll live to see anything like that ticker-tape parade again. Suddenly the twenty-seven years of suffering were twenty-seven minutes. They restored our pride."

All the joy and support from the trip would be needed to face the daunting tasks that awaited Nelson at home.

11 A NEW SOUTH AFRICA

Mandela faced three major problems: (1) negotiating a new form of government for South Africa, (2) solving the growing problem of violence between black groups, and (3) controlling the restless, impatient younger members of the ANC, who wanted a political solution that would allow black South Africans to rule the nation.

CHANGES IN SOUTH AFRICA

First was the daunting task of negotiations with de Klerk's government. It was clear to both sides that South Africa must make major changes in its political system. But the major questions remained: how great a change, and how soon?

In August 1990, in talks with government officials, the ANC agreed to suspend its policy of armed struggle. In return, the government would free political prisoners and allow exiles to return. It seemed as if both sides had won major concessions. But the government was not yet ready to release everyone who had committed acts of violence, even if they had been members of the ANC or other political groups. The ANC and the government began to argue over who was a political prisoner and who was not.

Thus, in December, when the ANC held its first national conference since being legalized, Mandela and the other leaders faced harsh criticism. Younger members felt that the leadership had made concessions in return for empty promises from the government.

The meeting was planned to be a joyous occasion. Oliver Tambo returned to the country after a thirty-year exile, bringing with him other leaders who had long been away. The delegates gave Tambo a warm, prolonged round of cheers as he appeared on the podium with Mandela at his side.

But it soon became clear that the grass-roots members of the ANC wanted to take a more militant stand than their elderly leaders proposed. The younger members, recruited secretly in the years when the older leaders were banned, were not committed to nonviolent struggle. They had lived in the South Africa of the "comrades," and had absorbed much of their spirit in believing that blacks should take what was rightfully theirs.

Mandela had to assert all his authority to keep the youthful agitators in line. In the end, the meeting confirmed the ANC's commitment to peaceful negotiations. But Mandela knew he had to take a hard line with the government in the future, if he were to keep the support of his followers.

De Klerk took a major step forward at the opening of Parliament on February 1, 1991. South Africa's president proclaimed that "the cornerstones of apartheid" would be dismantled. He said he would propose legislation to cancel the Land Acts of 1913 and 1936 and the Group Areas Act of 1966. These were the laws that had set aside 13 percent of the land for black citizens, and had forced them into homelands that would become independent of South Africa.

In addition, de Klerk announced his intention to repeal the Population Registration Act of 1950, which officially divided all citizens into one of the four racial groups. If carried out, this would end the hated pass system, in which blacks had to obtain permission to leave their designated areas.

Around the world, headlines proclaimed the end of apartheid. But it would not die as easily as many hoped. Even as de Klerk spoke, members of Parliament shouted, "Traitor!" and swore to resist his proposals. Forty-one members of the minority Conservative party walked out in protest.

Since de Klerk's National party controlled the Parliament, his proposals would be approved. Even so, South Africa's political system rested firmly on a racial basis. One of de Klerk's ministers said that the existing population register of races would have to remain in effect until a new constitution was written. This meant that blacks still could not vote, even in local elections. Coloreds and Indians would still vote for delegates to separate parliaments.

Furthermore, the fact remained that for decades blacks had been forcibly removed from lands that they once owned. Though they would now be allowed to buy land or houses anywhere, in fact most of them were too poor to do so. The government announced that houses in the black townships that were rented from the government would eventually be turned over to their occupants. But that would still leave them segregated into some of the nation's poorest areas.

AN ANNIVERSARY MESSAGE

Mandela was cautious about praising de Klerk's new proposals. Earlier, relations between the two men had cooled when Mandela accused the state security police of secretly aiding and encouraging Inkatha attacks on other blacks. He called the secret elements within the police "the third force," and accused de Klerk of bad faith.

A week after de Klerk's address to Parliament, Mandela held a press conference. It was the first anniversary of his release from prison. He said that he had been "very shocked" by the deterioration in black housing, education, health, and employment during the time he had been in jail. He warned that change would come slowly, and said again that he was not a "messiah."

Mandela asked other nations not to lift the economic sanctions against South Africa, despite de Klerk's steps to end apartheid. Nothing had yet been accomplished, and it was necessary to keep the pressure on the South African government. Mandela warned that if sanctions ended, he would lead "mass action," or protests that would discourage foreign businesses from resuming their activities in South Africa. Strikes, marches, consumer boycotts, and stay-at-homes would be used to push the black South African cause.

A reporter pointed out that South Africa's black population also suffered from foreign sanctions. South Africa's economic difficulties created high unemployment, and blacks were among those who lost their jobs. Mandela responded, "But this is the price we are prepared to pay in order to have a say in determining our own affairs."

Mandela wanted to strengthen his hand for the tough negotiations with the government that lay ahead. The most important issue would be the writing of a new constitution. Government officials now spoke of "power sharing." Mandela took that to mean that South Africa's 5 million whites would seek to maintain some kind of control over the nation's 33 million blacks. He could not accept that, saying, "It will not be easy to compromise on one person, one vote."

Such a formula would no doubt create a black-dominated government, since blacks far outnumbered the other racial groups in the country. Yet as Mandela himself acknowledged, many whites worried about their own fate under a black government. As one small-town Afrikaner said, "As I see the future of South Africa—with the rise of black power—you either have to speak Xhosa or German. You either stay here or you go back to Europe."

VIOLENCE OR PEACE?

Overshadowing the talks was the violence that had continued in black areas of the country. Mandela's public pleas for peace had no effect.

The worst violence was in Natal province. Zulus fought against Xhosas and also against other Zulus. Part of the Zulu–Xhosa dispute stemmed from the fact that Xhosas had moved from the arid Transkei into more fertile Zulu territory. In addition, the Zulus who supported Chief Buthelezi battled Zulus who backed the ANC and Mandela.

Buthelezi seemed to be Mandela's chief black rival, and many thought Buthelezi encouraged or tolerated the violence to embarrass Mandela. Buthelezi insisted that he be present at the bargaining table for any agreements on the future of the country. He was offended when the government talks with the ANC began without him. He wanted to preserve his own prestige and status as a leader equal in importance to Mandela.

Earlier, Buthelezi had boycotted the meeting between Mandela and the "homeland" leaders. In July 1990, Buthelezi transformed Inkatha into the Inkatha Freedom party, which he claimed had a membership of two million Zulus. This would make it at least equal to the ANC.

Violence between the two groups spread from Natal to the townships around Johannesburg, where Zulu migrant workers lived in hostels. By the end of 1990, almost five thousand people had been killed.

Mandela admitted that ANC supporters contributed to the violence. "There can be no denying that there have been instances of ANC supporters displaying intolerant behavior and at times even employing strong-arm methods to bully political rivals into silence," said Mandela in Cape Town on November 30, 1990. He added, "We want to take this opportunity to denounce in the strongest terms any such tactics as completely contrary to ANC policy."

Furthermore, the terrible conditions of poverty and inadequate education in the black townships had created an atmosphere of lawlessness in which violence was never far beneath the surface. On one weekend in January 1991, seventy-seven blacks were killed—forty of them in a riot at a soccer match, and thirty-five more when a gang fired automatic rifles into a crowd attending a funeral. The remaining two were found "necklaced"—burned to death, apparently in retaliation for the funeral attack.

Finally, Mandela and Buthelezi met face-to-face in a series of meetings. They appeared arm-in-arm, smiling. Mandela said, "I am happy . . . that we were able to take similar positions on a wide variety of issues." Publicly, each man urged his followers to stop the violence—yet it continued to plague the country. The country's leading black newspaper, *The Sowetan,* declared that the violence was "quite clearly, out of the control of any of these political leaders."

Solving this problem was particularly important, for whites pointed to the violence as evidence that blacks were unable to govern themselves. How then could blacks expect to assume an equal role in national politics?

THE WINNIE FACTOR

During all this time, Mandela had another burden—concern over his wife's future. The so-called "Winnie factor" threatened his own prestige. At the ANC meeting, some delegates openly criticized him for naming her to high leadership posts in the organization. Blacks had booed her even when she appeared with Nelson, for they had not forgotten or forgiven her alleged role in the murder of Stompie Moeketsi. Yet some black radicals admired her, for she held the same attitude toward black "traitors" as they had.

In May 1990, before the Mandelas' trip to the United States, Jerry Richardson, the former coach of Winnie's Football Club, was found guilty of Stompie's murder. He was sentenced to be hanged. The court had found that Winnie was present during some of the beatings of Stompie and the others. Witnesses described her as even having taken part in the beatings. The government could have brought Winnie to trial as well, but at first it did not.

Mandela stood by his wife. He deeply grieved that for over twenty-seven years he had not been able to protect her from the constant harassment to which she had been subjected. He criticized the government for not letting her prove her innocence in a trial. "My wife's whole reputation is being smashed without her having the opportunity to reply," he said.

During the Mandelas' world tour, few people brought up the subject of the Football Club's violence. Overseas, Winnie had for years been known for her courage and determination. Her name was permanently linked with Nelson's at the head of the South African freedom struggle.

But in September 1990, the government indicted Winnie on charges of kidnapping and assault. Nelson accompanied her to the courthouse. He stood stony-faced as the charge was read. Winnie announced that she welcomed the opportunity to clear her name in a "proper trial."

It is clear that Mandela blames himself for whatever Winnie may or may not have done. He knows that if he had not involved her in the freedom struggle, she would have carried out her ambition to serve others as a nurse and medical social worker. If he had left the country, taking her and his family, they could have lived elsewhere in peace. Facing the choice between the struggle for his people's freedom and the safety of his family, he chose freedom. Yet his conscience never let him forget the consequences of that choice for those he loved most.

THE TRIAL

Winnie's trial opened in February 1991. There was no jury. Instead, Judge Michael S. Stegmann both presided over the trial and decided the verdict. Besides Winnie, the defendants included seven other people, including members of the Football Club, Winnie's driver, and two women who lived near Winnie's house in Soweto. The prosecutor said he would show that Winnie and the others had taken part in several other kidnappings. He claimed that Winnie herself had taken part in the beatings of the four young men, which resulted in the death of Stompie Moeketsi.

The chief attorney for the defense was George Bizos, who had defended Nelson Mandela during the Rivonia trial. He read a statement from Winnie in which she denied taking part in the kidnappings or assaults. In fact, she said she had been out of town at the time the kidnapping had taken place.

The prosecutor startled the court when he announced that his first witness—one of the four young men who had been beaten at Winnie's house—had disappeared. The other two surviving victims were now afraid to testify.

After the police failed to find the missing witness, Judge Stegmann forced the other two to testify by threatening them with imprisonment if they did not do so. In early March, Kenneth Kgase took the stand. He said that Winnie had been present when he and the others were brought to her house and beaten. In fact, she had whipped and kicked them herself. The next day, Kgase and his companions had to wash their own blood off the walls of the room. Kgase said he escaped a few days later.

Stompie Moeketsi had been beaten worse than the others, Kgase said, because Winnie suspected him of being a police informer. When Jerry Richardson led Stompie out of the house, everyone could see he would not live long.

The second witness, Barend Thabiso Mono, confirmed Kgase's story. He said Winnie "hit me with open hands and fists on my face. After she assaulted us, all the people in there also started. . . . They were trampling on my body."

Yet Winnie and several other witnesses testified that she was in Brandfort on the night of the kidnapping. When she returned to Soweto, she was told that the four youths had been brought "voluntarily" to her home. She did not learn that they had been beaten until later.

On May 13, Judge Stegmann delivered his verdict. He described Winnie as "a calm, composed, deliberate, unblushing liar." He said it was "possibly true" that she had left for Brandfort after the kidnapping but before the beatings. However, she must have known about the beatings soon afterward, and then lied about her knowledge of them.

Judge Stegmann found Winnie guilty on the charges of kidnapping and of "accessory after the fact" to the beatings.

However, he cleared her of the more serious charge of taking part in the beatings herself.

Winnie emerged from the courthouse smiling and holding her fist high in triumph. She told a reporter, "As long as you all now know that I did not assault any child, that is all that matters to me." She said she was "delighted" by the verdict, but Nelson walked beside her, unsmiling and grim.

The next day Judge Stegmann sentenced Winnie to six years in jail. However, the case will be appealed, and it may be years before she has to serve her sentence. It is possible for President de Klerk to pardon her, but he did not comment on the matter during the trial.

HOPES FOR THE FUTURE

When Nelson Mandela left prison in February 1990, he was seventy-one years old. He resumed his life work with the vigor of a forty-year-old, setting a pace that tired out younger people who accompanied him. He seemed like a coiled spring, waiting for the chance to be allowed to lead his people and his nation to a new day of freedom.

No one knows how much time Mandela has. The question is a crucial one for South Africa. For only he commands the loyalty of enough black South Africans to guide the nation to a peaceful settlement of its long strife. Without his strong hand and spirit, South Africa might well erupt into a civil war that will cause enormous bloodshed.

Yet even he cannot solve all of the problems caused by the legacy of apartheid. A whole generation of young blacks has been poorly educated yet wants to take control of their nation. Neither poverty nor the results of a century of racism can simply be eradicated through any agreement that leaders make. And as we have seen, black South Africans have turned their anger against each other as well.

Furthermore, a sizable number of Afrikaners insist that they will not give up their privileged position without a fight.

Both Afrikaners and black South Africans have armed themselves for the struggle.

It may not have to be that way. In the neighboring country of Zimbabwe, a white minority voluntarily turned over power to a black government. The result was not bloodshed, but peace. Though some whites left Zimbabwe, most remained and have taken their places in a multiracial society like the one Mandela envisions for South Africa.

Only time will tell whether Mandela's struggle and sacrifice will in the end succeed. Someday we may see him as president of a united and free nation. For South Africa, this is the only solution that makes any sense. Yet people do not always choose peace over war, fairness over prejudice. The story of Nelson Mandela still has no ending.

And yet . . . the story will be told for a long time, for this man's life has marked him as truly great. In the face of an evil, repressive system, he seems never to have responded with hatred. A man who enjoyed all the pleasures of life, he suffered through twenty-seven years in prison. Yet his spirit was not destroyed or embittered. His unswerving determination and his desire for freedom have inspired his own people, and indeed the world.

SOURCE NOTES

INTRODUCTION
Page 9: "Our people . . ." *Facts on File*, June 29, 1990, p. 479.
Page 10: Mandela quotes, Dellums quote, Ibid.

CHAPTER 1: "I LISTENED TO THE ELDERS OF OUR TRIBE"
Page 12: "I am giving you . . ." Mary Benson, *Nelson Mandela,*
p. 17.
"He was shy . . ." Fatima Meer, *Higher Than Hope,* p. 7.
page 13: "Jongintaba was stern . . ." Ibid.
page 14: "People are people . . ." Allister Sparks, *The Mind of South Africa,* p. 4.
page 14: "I listened to . . ." Nelson Mandela, *The Struggle Is My Life,* p. 207.
page 18: "The South African . . ." Francis Meli, *A History of the ANC: South Africa Belongs to Us,* p. 4.
page 20: "The two of us . . ." Meer, *Higher Than Hope,* p. 9.

CHAPTER 2: A YOUNG MAN IN JOHANNESBURG
page 25: "We have no color bar . . ." Benson, *Nelson Mandela,* p. 24.

page 25: "You watch . . ." ibid., p. 24.
"the respect . . ." ibid., p. 25.
page 26: "very special about Nelson." Meer, *Higher Than Hope*, p. 40.
page 27: "The Congress Youth League . . ." N. Mandela, *The Struggle*, p. 17.
page 30: Policy statement, Ibid., p. 25.

CHAPTER 3: "NO EASY WALK TO FREEDOM"
page 34: "pleading their cause . . ." Benson, *Nelson Mandela*, p. 38.
page 35: "He has the natural air . . ." Nelson Mandela, *No Easy Walk to Freedom*, p. 11.
page 36: ANC letter, Benson, *Nelson Mandela*, pp. 44–45.
page 37: "I noticed people turning . . ." Ibid., p. 46.
page 39: "Who will deny . . ." Ronald Segal, *African Profiles*, pp. 31–32.
page 40: "to redouble . . ." N. Mandela, *The Struggle*, p. 40.
"You can see . . ." Ibid., p. 42.
"South African apartheid . . ." N. Mandela, *No Easy Walk*, p. 10.
page 41: "Every case . . ." Ibid., p. 10.
page 42: "If you could . . ." Benson, *Nelson Mandela*, p. 65.
"Large African grandmothers . . ." Anthony Sampson, *Treason Cage*, p. 106.
page 42: "We the people . . ." N. Mandela, *The Struggle*, p. 50.
page 45: "the two people . . ." Meer, *Higher Than Hope*, p. 79.
"He was the only man . . ." Ibid., p. 80.

CHAPTER 4: THE TREASON TRIAL
page 47: Signs, Benson, *Nelson Mandela*, p. 72.
page 48: "I became aware . . ." Winnie Mandela, *Part of My Soul Went with Him*, p. 46.
"She was literally . . ." Ibid., p. 47.
page 50: "Life with him . . ." Ibid., p. 59.
"You know . . ." Ibid., p. 59.
page 52: "was tantamount to . . ." Benson, *Nelson Mandela*, p. 82.
"these . . ." N. Mandela, *Winnie Mandela*, p. 63.
page 54: "serious threat . . ." Meer, *Higher Than Hope*, p. 150.
"until freedom has been won . . ." Ibid., p. 150.
page 54: "Prison regulations . . ." Benson, *Nelson Mandela*, p. 86.
page 55: "Yes, the Congress . . ." N. Mandela, *The Struggle*, p. 73.

page 55: "Well, as a matter of fact . . ." and Mandela reply. Ibid., p. 93.

page 55: Judge statement, W. Mandela, *Part of My Soul*, p. 68.

page 55: "There has never . . ." Ibid., p. 68.

CHAPTER 5: THE BLACK PIMPERNEL

page 59: "That was the last . . ." W. Mandela, *Part of My Soul*, p. 71.

page 60: "We have no illusions . . ." Benson, *Nelson Mandela*, p. 102.

"It is still not too late . . ." N. Mandela, *The Struggle*, p. 102.

page 60: "Heavy army vehicles . . ." Benson, *Nelson Mandela*, p. 103.

page 61: "I have had to . . ." N. Mandela, *The Struggle*, p. 115.

page 62: "I had so little . . ." W. Mandela, *Part of My Soul*, p. 72.

page 63: "We . . . have always sought . . ." Benson, *Nelson Mandela*, p. 110.

page 64: "Wherever I went . . ." Ibid., p. 114.

page 65: American newspaper . . . Manning, *"They Cannot Kill Us All"*, p. 167.

page 66: "I consider myself . . ." N. Mandela, *The Struggle*, p. 125.

"The government . . ." Benson, *Nelson Mandela*, p. 127.

page 66: "It has not been easy . . ." N. Mandela, *The Struggle*, pp. 148–149.

CHAPTER 6: A LIFE SENTENCE

page 68: "suffering in jail . . ." Benson, *Nelson Mandela*, p. 132.

page 71: "When you are the government . . ." Ibid., p. 136.

page 71: "The government . . ." Ibid., p. 138.

page 72: "Isn't Swanepoel . . ." Ibid., p. 142.

page 72: "I do not . . ." Ibid., p. 174.

"The African people . . ." N. Mandela, *The Struggle*, p. 158.

"I and some colleagues . . ." Ibid., p. 160.

page 73: "The ANC . . ." Benson, *Nelson Mandela*, p. 151.

"During my lifetime . . ." N. Mandela, *The Struggle*, p. 175.

page 75: "Here I was . . ." W. Mandela, *Part of My Soul*, p. 82.

CHAPTER 7: PRISONER NUMBER 446/64

page 78: "Do you know . . ." N. Mandela, *The Struggle*, p. 180.

"Nelson is . . ." Ibid., p. 194.

"You begin the task . . ." Meer, *Higher Than Hope*, p. 266.

page 78: "worse than fear..." W. Mandela, *Part of My Soul,* p. 85.
page 80: "I don't know..." Ibid., p. 86.
page 83: "There, pray..." Nancy Harrison, *Winnie Mandela,* p. 118.
page 84: "I am solidly..." Meer, *Higher Than Hope,* p. 301.

CHAPTER 8: A NAME THAT WOULD NOT DIE
page 86: "to break the human spirit..." Meer, *Higher Than Hope,* p. 268.
"Locked up by yourself..." Ibid., p. 268.
page 87: "Surely you can see..." Benson, *Nelson Mandela,* p. 181.
"But remember..." Meer, *Higher Than Hope,* p. 354.
page 90: "I saw a stream..." Harrison, *Winnie Mandela,* p. 133.
page 91: "The Boers..." Richard Manning, *"They Cannot Kill Us All": An Eyewitness Account of South Africa Today,* p. 83.
page 92: "I was more radical..." Meer, *Higher Than Hope,* p. 273.
"He did as we..." Ibid., p. 272.
page 93: "I would have..." W. Mandela, *Part of My Soul,* p. 137.
page 94: Poem, from *Black As I Am* (Los Angeles: Guild of Tutors Press of International College, 1978.)
"On some days..." Meer, *Higher Than Hope,* pp. 277–278.

CHAPTER 9: FREE MANDELA!
page 101: "There was no..." *Current Biography Yearbook,* 1986, p. 78.
pages 101: "My father says..." W. Mandela, *Part of My Soul,* pp. 146–148.
page 102: "It was only then..." Ibid.
page 103: "Unlike white people..." Samuel Dash, "A Rare Talk with Nelson Mandela," *New York Times Magazine,* July 7, 1985, p. 20.
"On occasions like this..." Benson, *Nelson Mandela,* pp. 237–238.
page 104: "Together, hand in hand..." Graham Boynton, "How Bad Is Winnie Mandela?" *Vanity Fair,* October 1990, p. 234.
page 106: "most scandalous persec̲u̲t̲i̲o̲n̲..." ̲ ̲ ̲ ̲ ̲ ̲ ̲ ̲ ̲ ̲ ̲ ̲ ̲ ̲ Dau,
page 106: "Those who visited..." Ibid., p. 322.
page 107: "I only would like..." Rebecca Stefoff, *Nelson Mandela: A Voice Set Free,* p. 119.
"the only way..." Ibid., p. 120.

CHAPTER 10: FREEDOM

page 108: "the man with..." *Current Biography,* February 1990, p. 22.

page 109: "White domination..." Ibid., p. 22.

page 109: "The season of violence..." *Facts on File,* February 9, 1990, p. 78.

page 111: "a humble servant..." *Facts on File,* February 16, 1990, p. 98.

page 112: "The hijacking and..." *Facts on File,* February 16, 1990, p. 100.

page 113: "Hang de Klerk..." *Time,* February 19, 1990, p. 43.
"Take your guns..." *Facts on File,* March 2, 1990, p. 136.

page 113: "We have reached..." Ibid.

page 114: "This is the first..." *Facts on File,* May 11, 1990, p. 337.

page 116: "I saw Mandela..." *Time,* July 2, 1990, p. 17.

page 116: "From behind..." Ibid., p. 18.

page 117: "I am here..." Ibid., p. 16.

page 118: "I don't think..." Boynton, "How Bad," p. 242.

CHAPTER 11: A NEW SOUTH AFRICA

page 120: "the cornerstones..." *Washington Post,* February 2, 1991, p. 1.

page 121: Mandela quotes, *Washington Post,* February 10, 1991, p. A14.

page 122: "But this is..." *New York Times,* February 9, 1991, p. 3.
"It will not..." *Christian Science Monitor,* February 11, 1991, p. 4.
"As I see..." Ibid., February 15, 1991, p. 6.

page 123: "There can be..." *New York Times,* December 5, 1990, p. A3.
"I am happy..." *Washington Post,* March 31, 1991, p. A17.

page 124: "quite clearly..." *New York Times,* March 31, 1991, p. 3.

page 125: "My wife's whole reputation..." *Christian Science Monitor,* October 9, 1990, p. 5.
"proper trial." Ibid.

page 126: "hit me with..." *Washington Post,* March 14, 1991, p. A27.

page 126 insert: Stegmann quotes, Winnie Mandela quotes, *Washington Post,* May 14, 1991, p. A1.

BIBLIOGRAPHY

Benson, Mary. *Nelson Mandela.* New York: W. W. Norton, 1986.

Breytenbach, Breyten. *End Papers.* New York: Farrar, Straus and Giroux, 1986.

Denoon, Donald, and Balam Nyeko. *Southern Africa since 1800.* London: Longman, 1984.

Harrison, Nancy. *Winnie Mandela.* New York: George Braziller, 1986.

Hoobler, Dorothy, and Thomas Hoobler. *Nelson and Winnie Mandela.* New York: Franklin Watts, 1987.

Malan, Rian. *My Traitor's Heart.* New York: Atlantic Monthly Press, 1990.

Mandela, Nelson. *No Easy Walk to Freedom.* London: Heinemann, 1965.

Mandela, Nelson. *The Struggle* ....national ... and Aid Fund for Southern Africa, 1978.

Mandela, Winnie. *Part of My Soul Went with Him.* New York: W. W. Norton, 1984.

134

Manning, Richard. *"They Cannot Kill Us All": An Eyewitness Account of South Africa Today.* Boston: Houghton Mifflin, 1987.

Maquet, Jacques. *Civilizations of Black Africa.* New York: Oxford University Press, 1972.

Meer, Fatima. *Higher Than Hope.* New York: Harper & Row, 1988.

Meli, Francis. *A History of the ANC: South Africa Belongs to Us.* Bloomington, IN: Indiana University Press, 1989.

Russell, Diana E. H. *Lives of Courage: Women for a New South Africa.* New York: Basic Books, 1989.

Sampson, Anthony. *Treason Cage.* London: Heinemann, 1955.

Segal, Ronald. *African Profiles.* Baltimore: Penguin Books, 1962.

Sparks, Allister. *The Mind of South Africa.* New York: Knopf, 1990.

Stefoff, Rebecca. *Nelson Mandela: A Voice Set Free.* New York: Fawcett Columbine, 1990.

Stengel, Richard. *January Sun, One Day, Three Lives in A South African Town.* New York: Simon & Schuster, 1990.

Tessendorf, K. C. *Along the Road to Soweto: A Racial History of South Africa.* New York: Atheneum, 1989.

Woods, Donald. *Biko.* New York: Henry Holt, 1987.

FOR FURTHER READING

Many books about Nelson Mandela are now available. Some are listed below. Remember that Mandela is only one of many people who have worked for equality among the racial groups in South Africa. The story of the struggle for freedom in South Africa is a long and complex one.

Benson, Mary. *Nelson Mandela.* New York: W. W. Norton, 1986.

Hoobler, Dorothy, and Thomas Hoobler. *Nelson and Winnie Mandela.* New York: Franklin Watts, 1987.

Malan, Rian. *My Traitor's Heart.* New York: Atlantic Monthly Press, 1990.

Mandela, Nelson. *No Easy Walk to Freedom.* London: Heinemann, 1965.

Mandela, Nelson. *The Struggle Is My Life.* London: International Defense and Aid, 1978.

Mandela, Winnie. *Part of My Soul Went with Him.* New York: W. W. Norton, 1984.

Manning, Richard. *"They Cannot Kill Us All": An Eyewitness Account of South Africa Today.* Boston: Houghton Mifflin, 1987.

Meer, Fatima. *Higher Than Hope.* New York: Harper & Row, 1988.

Stefoff, Rebecca. *Nelson Mandela: A Voice Set Free.* New York: Fawcett Columbine, 1990.

Index

Africanists, 43, 52
African National Congress
  (ANC), 18, 26–28, 30, 31,
  34–40, 42, 43, 47, 52–54,
  57–58, 61–65, 70, 72, 83,
  88, 100–103, 109–115,
  117–120, 123, 124
Afrikaans, 17, 83, 89
Afrikaner Nationalist Party
  (ANP), 32, 107–109, 112, 121
Afrikaners, 16, 17, 24, 29, 32,
  108, 109, 122, 127–128 (see
  also Boers)
All-in-African Conference
  (1961), 59
Apartheid
  changes in, 98–101
  definition of, 32
  dismantling of, 120–121
  effects of, 40–41
  program of, 32–33, 37
Arafat, Yasir, 117

Banning, 39–40, 51, 55, 58

Bantu Education Act (1953), 33
Bantustans policy, 57–58, 85
Biko, Steve, 88, 90
Bizos, George, 125–126
Black Consciousness, 88–92
Blood River, Battle of (1838),
  16, 63
Boers, 16–17, 22 (see also
  Afrikaners)
Boer War (1899–1902), 17–18
Boesak, Allan, 99
Botha, Pieter W., 101, 106–108
Bush, George, 117
Buthelezi, Mangosuthu Gatsha,
  101, 112, 113, 115, 123, 124

Cape Coloreds, 16, 24,
  28
Cape of Good Hope, 11, 15–16
Cape Province, 17, 19
Castro, Fidel, 117
Censorship, 34
Chartists, 43
Civil disobedience, 35, 38

Communist party of South Africa, 29, 34, 35, 110
"Comrades" (*amadla kufa*), 104, 105, 112, 113
Congress Alliance, 42–43
Conservative party of South Africa, 112, 115, 121

Dash, Samuel, 102–103
Day of the Covenant, 16
Defiance Campaign (1952), 36–39, 41, 47
De Klerk, Frederik Willem, 108–110, 112–115, 119–122, 127
De Klerk, Jan, 108
De Klerk, Willem, 109
Dellums, Ronald, 10
Dinkins, David, 115–117
Disinvestment, 100
Divestiture, 100
Dutch East India Company, 15

Fischer, Bram, 29
Fort Hare College, 19–20, 24, 41
Freedom Charter, 41–43, 46, 47, 49, 56, 105
"Free Mandela" movement, 96–97

Gandhi, Mohandas ("Mahatma"), 28, 35, 36
Group Areas Act (1966), 33, 120

Homelands policy, 33, 57–58, 101, 114
Huguenots, 15

Indians, 16, 22, 24, 25, 28, 29, 38, 121

Inkatha Freedom party, 101, 112, 113, 115, 121, 123

Jan Hofmeyr School of Social Work, 49
Johannesburg, 14, 17, 19–22, 29, 40, 49
Johannesburg Stock Exchange, 53
Jongintaba, Chief of Thembus, 12–13, 19, 20, 23, 37

Kgase, Kenneth, 126
Khaddafi, Muammar, 117
Khois (Hottentots), 15
King, Martin Luther, Jr., 117
KwaZulu, 101

Lafayette, Marquis de, 9
Land Acts (1913 and 1936), 120
Lilliesleaf Farm, 61, 64, 70
London University, 73
Luthuli, Albert, 37–39, 43, 46–48, 53, 62, 64, 81

Madikizela, Columbus, 48, 51, 58
Madikizela, Gertrude, 48
Madikizela, Nom Zamo Winnie, See, Mandela, Nomzamo Winnie
Malan, Daniel, 32, 36–37, 101
Malcolm X, 117
Mandela, Evelyn Ntoko (Mase), 26, 30, 31, 35, 43–45, 83
Mandela, Hendry Gadla, 12–13
Mandela, Leabie, 30, 45
Mandela, Makgatho, 35, 44, 55,

Mandela, Nelson Rolihlahla ("Buti")
  African heritage and, 14

African National Congress
and, 26, 27, 31, 34, 113, 120

All-in-African Conference
and, 59

anniversary speech of, 121–122

arrests of, 38, 46, 65

banning orders on, 40, 51, 55, 58

Bantustans policy and, 58

Botha and, 106–107

Buthelezi and, 123, 124

children and, 44, 78, 79, 82–83, 93, 112

civil disobedience and, 35, 38

Defiance Campaign and, 36–38, 41

De Klerk and, 110, 112–115, 121

early years of, 12–15

education of, 12–13, 19–20, 25, 28–29, 31, 40, 87–88

Freedom Charter and, 43

friends and, 19–20

future for, 127, 128

illnesses of, 106

as lawyer, 40, 41, 52, 55

marriage to Evelyn, 26, 44–45

marriage to Winnie, 50–51, 78–79, 83–84, 93, 103, 105–106, 124–125

moves to Johannesburg, 20–23

Nehru Prize awarded to, 96

in prison, 68–69, 76–78, 81–88, 91–95, 97–98, 101–103, 106

release from prison, 110–113

religion and, 12, 29

Soweto massacre and, 91

Spear of the Nation and, 62–65, 67, 70, 72, 73

speech to United States Congress, 9, 10, 117

trials of, 9, 46–48, 51–52, 54–56, 66–67, 70–75

visits United States, 115–118

work underground, 59–62

world tour of, 9, 113–118

Youth League and, 30, 35

Mandela, Nosekeni Fanny, 12, 30, 31, 44, 45, 74, 81

Mandela, Thembi, 30, 31, 44, 45, 82

Mandela, Nomzamo Winnie (Madikizela), 48, 52, 54–56, 58, 59, 61–62, 65, 74–75, 80, 87, 88, 92–93, 97–99, 101, 106, 110, 116, 118

banning order on, 79

Black Consciousness and, 89, 90

early years of, 48

education of, 48–49

Mandela Football Club and, 104–106, 124–125

marriage to Nelson, 50–51, 78–79, 83–84, 93, 103, 105–106, 124–125

in prison, 81–83

trial of, 125–127

Mandela, Zenani ("Zeni"), 52, 74, 79, 80–82, 93, 96–98

Mandela Zindziswa ("Zindzi"), 56, 74, 79, 80, 82, 93, 94, 101, 106

Mandela Football Club, 104–106, 124, 125

Matanzima, George, 51, 57
Matanzima, Kaiser, 19–20, 51, 57, 58, 85
Matthews, Z. K., 41
Meer, Ismail, 28, 29
Mines, 18, 22, 29–30
Moeketsi Seipei, James ("Stompie"), 105, 124–126
Mono, Barend Thabiso, 126
Motlana, Nthato, 89, 90
M Plan, 40

Natal Province, 16, 22, 28, 37, 64, 112, 115, 123
National party of South Africa, 32, 107–109, 112, 121
Native Representative Council, 37
"Necklacing," 99, 104, 124
Ngubengcuka, King, 12

Operation T, 46
Orange Free State, 17, 92, 105

Pan African Freedom Conference, 63
Pan Africanist Congress (PAC), 52–54, 58, 70, 88, 110
Parliament of South Africa, 18, 27, 109, 115, 120, 121
Pass system, 18–19, 52–53, 120
Plaatje, Solomon, 18
Pollsmoor Prison, 97–98, 101, 104, 106
Pondoland, 19, 48, 51, 58
Population Registration Act (1950), 32, 120
Pretoria, 51–52
Pretoria Central Prison, 68, 82, 90
Program of Action, 34

Radebe, Gaur, 25

Reserves, 12, 18–19, 33, 57
Richardson, Jerry, 124, 126
Riebeeck, Jan van, 15
Rivonia trial, 70–73, 97
Robben Island prison, 68–70, 76–78, 81, 83, 86–87, 90, 91, 97, 98, 106
Robeson, Paul, 117

Sanctions, economic, 10, 53, 100–101, 115–117, 122
Sans (Bushmen), 15
Sharpeville massacre (1960), 53, 57
Sisulu, Albertina, 79
Sisulu, Walter, 24–27, 34, 35, 38, 43, 44, 46, 59, 70, 97, 98, 109, 111
Slavery, 15–17
Slovo, Joe, 29
Smuts, Jan Christiaan, 22
Sobukwe, Robert, 52–53, 69–70, 88
South African Students' Organization (SASO), 88
South African Youth Congress, 111
Soweto (Southwest township), 30, 44, 49, 51, 79, 89, 91, 103–104, 111, 112
Soweto massacre, 88–91
Spear of the Nation (Umkhonto we Sizwe), 62–65, 67, 69, 70, 72, 73
Stegmann, Michael S., 125, 126
Strijdom, Johannes, 108
Sugarcane plantations, 16, 22, 28
Suppression of Communism Act (1950), 33–34, 38
Supreme Court of South Africa, 41, 83
Swanepoel, 71–72
Swaziland, 80, 93

142

Tambo, Oliver, 19, 26, 27, 35,
  36, 40–41, 46, 48, 50,
  52–54, 63, 113, 114, 120
Thembu people, 12
Townships, 23, 24, 33
Transkei, 11–12, 18, 23, 24, 26,
  30, 48, 51, 57, 58, 85, 123
Transvaal, 17, 22, 31, 34, 35, 40
Treason Trial, 46–48, 51–52,
  54–55
Treaty of Vereeniging (1902), 18
Tsukudu, Adelaide, 50
Tutu, Desmond, 99–100

Umtata, 12
United Democratic Front
  (UDF), 99, 101
United Nations, 53, 74

University of natal, 88
University of South Africa, 25
University of Witwatersrand,
  25, 28, 105

Verwoerd, Hendrik, 60
Victor Verster Prison, 106, 110
Voting rights, 18, 27, 30, 114,
  121

Walesa, Lech, 9
World War II, 22, 27

Xhosa people, 11–14, 24, 123

Youth League, 27, 30, 31, 34

Zulus, 16, 37, 39, 123

143